Pisces

20 February – 20 March

First published in Great Britain 2009
by Harlequin Mills & Boon Limited,
Eton House, 18-24 Paradise Road, Richmond, Surrey TW9 1SR

Copyright © Dadhichi Toth 2008 & 2009

ISBN: 978 0 263 87075 6

Typeset at Midland Typesetters Australia

Harlequin Mills & Boon policy is to use papers that are natural, renewable and recyclable products and made from wood grown in sustainable forests. The logging and manufacturing processes conform to the legal environmental regulations of the country of origin.

Printed and bound in Spain
by Litografia Rosés S.A., Barcelona

About
Dadhichi

Dadhichi is one of Australia's foremost astrologers. He has the ability to draw from complex astrological theory to provide clear, easily understandable advice and insights for people who want to know what their future might hold.

In the 26 years that Dadhichi has been practising astrology, face reading and other esoteric studies, he has conducted over 9,500 consultations. His clients include celebrities, political and diplomatic figures, and media and corporate identities from all over the world.

Dadhichi's unique blend of astrology and face reading helps people fulfil their true potential. His extensive experience practising western astrology is complemented by his research into the theory and practice of eastern systems of astrology.

Dadhichi features in numerous newspapers and magazines and he also appears regularly on many of Australia's leading television and radio networks, where many of his political and worldwide forecasts have proved uncannily accurate.

His website www.astrology.com.au is now one of the top ten online Australian lifestyle sites and, in conjunction with www.facereader.com, www.soulconnector.com and www.psychjuice.com, they attract over half a million visitors monthly. The websites offer a wide variety of features, helpful information and personal services.

Dedicated to The Light of Intuition

Sri V. Krishnaswamy— mentor and friend

With thanks to Julie, Joram, Isaac and Janelle

Welcome from
Dadhichi

Dear Friend,

Welcome! It's great to have you here, reading your horoscope, trying to learn more about yourself and what's in store for you in 2010.

I visited Mexico a while ago and stumbled upon the Mayan prophecies for 2012, which, they say, is the year when the longstanding calendar we use in the western world supposedly stops! If taken literally, some people could indeed believe that 'the end of the world is near'. However, I see it differently.

Yes, it might seem as though the world is getting harder and harder to deal with, especially when fear enters our lives. But, I believe that 'the end' indicated by these Mayan prophecies has more to do with the end that will create new beginnings for our societies, more to do with making changes to our material view of life and some necessary adjustments for the human race to progress and prosper in future. So let's get one thing straight: you and I will both be around after 2012, reading our 2013 horoscopes!

My prediction and advice centres around keeping a cool mind and not reacting to the fear that could overtake us. Of course, this isn't easy, especially when media messages might increase our anxiety about such things as the impacts of global warming or the scarcity of fossil fuels.

I want you to understand that it is certainly important to be aware and play your part in making the world a better place; however, the best and surest way to support global goals is to help yourself first. Let me explain. If everyone focused just a little more on improving *themselves* rather than just pointing their finger to criticise others, it would result in a dramatic change and improvement; not just globally, but societally. And, of course, you mustn't forget what a positive impact this would have on your personal relationships as well.

Astrology focuses on self-awareness; your own insights into your personality, thinking processes and relationships. This is why this small book you have in your hand doesn't only concentrate on what is going to happen, but more importantly how you can *make* things happen positively through being your best.

I have always said that there are two types of people: puppets and actors. The first simply react to each outside stimulus and are therefore slaves of their environment, and even of their own minds and emotions. They are puppets in the hands of karma. The other group I call actors. Although they can't control what happens to them all the time, either, they are better able to adapt and gain something purposeful in their lives. They are in no way victims of circumstance.

I hope you will use what is said in the following pages to become the master of your destiny, and not rely on the predictions that are given as mere fate but as valuable guidelines to use intelligently when life presents you with its certain challenges.

Neither the outside world, nor the ups and downs that occur in your life, should affect your innermost spirituality and self-confidence. Take control: look beyond your current challenges and use them as the building blocks of experience to create success and fulfilment in the coming year.

I believe you have the power to become great and shine your light for all to see. I hope your 2010 horoscope book will be a helpful guide and inspiration for you.

Warm regards, and may the stars shine brightly for you in 2010!

Your Astrologer,

Dadhichi Toth

Contents

The Pisces
Identity

What happens is not as important as how you react to what happens.

—Thaddeus Golas

Pisces: A Snapshot

Key Characteristics

Sympathetic, perceptive, intuitive, spiritual, dreamy, confused, inspired

Compatible Star Signs

Cancer, Taurus, Scorpio and Capricorn

Key Life Phrase

I sacrifice

Life Goals

Self-knowledge and true, unconditional love

Platinum Assets

Tireless and selfless worker, powerful intuitive gifts

Zodiac Totem

The Fish

Zodiac Symbol

♊

13

Zodiac Facts

Twelfth sign of the zodiac; mutable, fruitful,
feminine, moist

Element

Water

Famous Pisceans

Kurt Cobain, Karen Carpenter, Alan Greenspan,
Albert Einstein, Ariel Sharon, Carrot Top, David Niven,
Dr Seuss, George Washington, Glenn Close,
Gordon Brown, Ivan Lendl, Jerry Lewis,
George Harrison, Johnny Cash, Kathy Ireland,
Ron Howard, Rupert Murdoch

Pisces: Your profile

There's an innate wisdom and commonsense
attached to the symbolism of astrology. The totems
and animals represented by the twelve signs
throughout history aptly reflect the character and
life traits of those born under these stars.

Pisces, you are ruled by the fish. And not just
any old fish, but two fish, swimming in diametrically
opposed directions. Speaking of just how well you
are described by this totem, we would have to say
'perfectly', Pisces.

You are indeed a most unusual person, living
between two conflicting paths most of the time.
One of the fish swims one way and the other fish
swims contrary to it. This is like your mind moving

away from your heart, so choosing your directions in life will often not be easy. Such opposing pairs as sacrifice versus self-interest, or idealism versus practicality, very much represent your Piscean mind-and-heart dilemmas.

Throughout this deep, inner longing to find the right balance between any two extremes, you will reach out in your idealism and draw others in need towards you. This is because your natural inclination is to help by serving and enlightening anyone and everyone.

If you can't find 'perfect peace' right now, so be it. You'll end up helping others find their own equanimity, peace and sublime love until it is your own turn. Also, you believe in the doctrine of karma; that is, by helping others in this way, in turn you are helping yourself.

You are soft, sensitive and actually quite unafraid to explore what life offers you, even if you choose actions, people and circumstances that convention normally frowns upon. You understand that finding your ideals could involve exploring things traditionally regarded as taboo. But you would rather do this than die wondering 'What if ... ?'.

You're not primarily motivated by money, but this doesn't mean you're not interested in it. To you money is a form of energy, a measure of your own activity and love to be used in helping others, possibly even uplifting humanity in some way. Even in your ordinary tasks you're quick to grasp an opportunity to be of assistance. Friend or stranger alike, you're always on the lookout for opportunities to relieve the suffering of others.

Your psychic energies are supremely developed. Always trust your intuition, Pisces. Being born under this sign means you have evolved to an extraordinary height. You are tuned in to people in a way that supersedes typical mental or verbal communication. You are clairvoyant, channelling the highest spiritual truth for yourself and others during this life.

With your highly developed sensitivity comes creativity and artistic flair as well as an eye for beauty and harmony. Having a strong love of nature means you easily connect with the wonders of the world around you. You have a tremendous respect for the majesty of life and all of its expressions, particularly in artistic objects and music.

The less-evolved Pisceans struggle with their paths. If hurt or disillusioned by life's complex stream of events, then they withdraw. If you happen to be one of these Piscean types, I offer a special message of hope to hang in there and don't identify too much with your past story. Extend yourself to others; help the downtrodden and those who are suffering. You may not immediately unravel the mystery of what is happening to you, but this path of self-surrender is the perfect tool for gradually removing your own pain.

Your Piscean sign is a water sign, which reflects your caring and loving attitude. You are a true friend and now stand on the threshold of the deepest wisdom possible, having evolved through all the other signs of the zodiac.

Your mission is to give unconditional love to all you come in touch with, and eventually rise to the occasion to meet your higher self—a feat few other star signs are capable of.

Three classes of Pisces

Those of you born between the 20th and the 28th or 29th of February are very powerfully ruled by Neptune, the god of the oceans. This means you are extremely tuned in to psychic and clairvoyant realms and will have a natural desire to seek out spiritual information. You are a born social worker and even if you don't work in this arena specifically you will always be available to help others solve their problems.

If you happen to be born between the 1st and 10th of March, you love people but are particularly attached to your kith and kin and excel in sharing your love in close personal relationships. You are loyal and make everyone feel comfortable in your company.

As a Pisces born between the 11th and 20th of March you have a streak of Scorpio in your nature that makes you passionate, demanding and very intense. A 100 per cent response from others is rarely enough for you, so you need to be careful of not being too possessive or jealous in your relationships.

Pisces role model: Ron Howard

Ron Howard, the famous director whose character was Ritchie in the early TV series Happy Days
expresses true Piscean ideals. Working in film is a
natural fit for a Pisces. With Ron's productions, you
will see his messages are always about the mysteri-
ous, beautiful, compassionate and spiritual sides
of life. You could say that Ron is endeavouring to
share his inner spiritual wisdom with the world
through his filmmaking.

Pisces: The light side

Pisces, you are able to draw others to you: this
is one of your greatest strengths. Being ruled by
Neptune makes you dreamy and enigmatic in the
way you are able to attract others. When someone
is drawn to you they can't quite figure out why, but
they love you, anyway. You genuinely care for others
and have a transparency that people trust. You are
honest in your love and strive to live the ideal of
unconditional giving.

You're an adjustable person. You have no
problem—just like water, your ruling element—
in assuming the shape of whatever container it's
placed in. You have the uncanny knack of adapting
to circumstances and people wherever you find
yourself. You'll be admired for your ability to capitalise on situations due to this.

You have an inner beauty that's hard to pinpoint,
and this has nothing to do with your physical looks.

You radiate a spirit of love and you do genuinely care for people. Come to think of it, even strangers feel as if they know you. You relax people and make them feel as if they're part of your family.

Being sociable by nature, you share your insights with others and truly help many in your life. You are a blessing to humanity.

Pisces: The shadow side

Please don't let emotions dominate your life. There are deep parts of your nature that you suppress only to find them resurfacing in ways you often can't deal with. When this happens you are prone to try to escape from a 'reality' you can't understand. If this happens, I can't emphasise strongly enough the need for you to avoid the temptation to indulge in alcohol or other mind-altering drugs.

Pisces is a complex personality, to say the least, and for this reason you should take care when dealing with the kaleidoscope of emotional colours that emanate from within you. Your sensitivity and depth of emotion can quickly change from positive to pessimistic if you're not careful. You need to be watchful of things that will trigger your moodiness, making it get the better of you. Spend some time each day thinking about how you can redirect your powers into positive channels that will help others as well as yourself.

You must never be impulsive without giving due thought to the issues at hand. You're likely to rely on your intuition, which is excellent, but not always 100 per cent correct. Assuming people are better than they are is one such thing that needs due diligence on your part. Using your mind rather than your heart is essential when dealing with the real world. This will spare you all sorts of upheavals down the track.

Pisces woman

You are born under Pisces, which means you are a special human being. Elegance. That's the Piscean woman in a nutshell. This sums up your character, which is uniquely gentle and sensitive. Just like the deep ocean that your ruling planet Neptune represents, there's a depth and grace not easily matched by females of any other star sign. It's not at all in your nature to be hard or ruthless and your softness attracts people to you throughout your life.

Words are not necessary for a Piscean woman because her demeanour, presence and even a casual glance express her personality in a most dignified way. The Piscean woman is truly the quintessential combination of the sensual and the mystical. Because Pisces is a feminine sign, you embody the ideals of women generally.

Pisces women have powerful imaginations. You can conjure up what you want. Don't underestimate your Neptunian powers, the forces of your ruling planet, which make things happen almost as if by magic.

Pisces is a truly magical sign that few rarely understand. Truly speaking, you may not even understand yourself. But at some stage you will discover there is a magic power within you; perhaps you already did when you were young. It is the power to dream.

There are times when your desire in nature is so strong that you become blinkered in making those dreams come true. You deeply care about others, but must consider the ramifications and the consequences of your desire to fulfil these deep longings of your heart. Manifesting your Piscean dreams may come at a price.

You will realise that the more intense your goals are, the bigger the sacrifices you might need to make to achieve them. And you could possibly even give up everything in your life for these ideals. Why else would some deeply spiritual monks and other reclusive types fall under the astrological banner of Pisces? Yes, your sacrifices may involve money, even members of the opposite sex, family, power ... perhaps everything!

Pisces women who don't give up everything in their world still carry with them incredibly super-psychic powers. You intuitively know what others think, especially when people are trying to fool you. So how odd is it that, even knowing this, you still allow yourself to be exploited? Here we go again with your notion of seeing the best in others (this is a skewed version of what it should be).

Pisces women have vision, extraordinary imaginations they wish to express in every part of their lives. Sometimes others will find it somewhat difficult to deal with you. Likewise, you find it puzzling as to why people don't immediately understand your ideas. They seem to look at you in such a way as to wonder why they are so impractical. It's just that your visions are probably years ahead of their time.

Piscean women are extremely sociable as well as artistic. You like the idea of combining creativity with fun, and cultural activities capture your imagination. Venus, the goddess of love, is exalted in your Sun sign. The female Piscean is the goddess of love incarnate.

You are idealistic in the way you approach your relationships and are flexible as well, but you must learn when to 'bed down' and commit. Please don't confuse personal sacrifice with an endless series of dilemmas that are actually masquerades for your commitment phobia.

Try to keep yourself active and don't drown yourself in negative thoughts or self-defeating behaviour. Alcohol is not advisable, even in moderate amounts. You may find it all too easy to rely on substances to help you overcome your problems in life.

Pisces man

Pisces men are as sensitive and intuitive as females born under this sign. Not only are you not afraid to admit your strong affinity with the feminine side of your being, but openly advocate the beauty and satisfaction you feel with this inner connection.

You could truly be classed as a SNAG, a Sensitive New Age Guy.

Yours is the dual water sign of two fish swimming in opposite directions. The fish represent your inner desires and self. These two little sea creatures could even be trying to avoid each other. Perhaps the reason why they are repelling each other is to show you exactly what is happening in yourself. What are you hiding or running away from?

The Pisces male travels a roundabout path in life if he fails to accept his own weaknesses and rise above them. Consider this as the true meaning of the two-way symbol. You have the power of pure love oozing from the core of your soul. Overcoming your life issues rests on this one strength. By helping others where you can, you will soon discover the secret of your inner ability. It is the unconditional, selfless load of giving that ultimately lifts you to the next level. Yes, the Pisces man is the ultimate helper.

Occasionally you appear to be so self-absorbed and inwardly engaged that people, especially colleagues, find you strange. You tend to 'zone out' and this can be mistaken for either a lack of interest or arrogance on your part. Actually, you're a creative person and are often thinking about things with such concentration that you completely tune out to everything around you. It's a form of 'meditation in action' that seems to be part and parcel of who you are.

You might like to explain to others that it's not anything personal. It's because of this ability that you're able to tap into areas of human nature accessible to only a few, including yourself. As a result, you're able to create original work and come up with various unusual ideas. If you're involved in a creative vocation, you're apt to be rather brilliant.

Unfortunately you tend to be idealistic about people and life as a whole. Unscrupulous people often find you an easy target and can spin a hard luck story that you'll believe. You take people at face value and on more than one occasion will have found yourself being taken advantage of, perhaps even losing money, not to mention pride.

Sexual partners are drawn to you and you like to explore this. You don't worry that others see you as unconventional in this respect, either. Even if you are married or committed, you'll wear a discreet 'mask' to manage this seemingly conventional side of your life while at the same time never denying your personal needs—understanding your drives— whether they are dark or light.

As you grow in age and wisdom, your self-satisfaction will eventually pull you away from the lure of the world at large and all its pleasures. 'This is your last time around', as they say in karma-speak. The Piscean man is, after all, primarily concerned with his evolution, selfless love and the higher progress of humanity, even if for a while in his youth he daringly sought the Earthly pleasures of life as well.

Pisces child

Your Pisces child could be a little unsettling, especially because from their early infancy you get a sense of their higher power and knowledge. In some ways they will assume the role of parent and guru in the manner of their understanding.

This understanding is pure and comes from a deeply caring part of them. They know how to love without being taught. They know how to share without instruction and compassion. You'll see a tear trickle down their cheek the instant they spy suffering in even the dumbest of creatures.

Your Pisces child seems to be connected to the whole of nature. They are lovers of the outdoors, of all animals, large and small. You must give them a pet for their birthday at some stage. This will bring out their best flavour and also teach you the true meaning of love and affection.

Pisces children need continual grounding. Discipline will be difficult if you are the parent of a Piscean child. Their highly sensitive nature makes them prone to withdrawing from the world around them and, if they feel they've been unfairly punished, this could become a serious issue.

Even if you realise they have to be raised with certain standards and a measure of discipline, try to remember that their sensitive little beings can't deal with heavy handed punishment. The trick will be to find the right balance between fairness and discipline.

You might also sometimes find them mentally 'floating in air' or staring into nothing. This is their way to zone out and allow the subtle forces of nature to flow through them. When you notice this, don't interrupt them too abruptly.

Allow them those special moments to connect with other realms, but also balance them with bouts of sport, of focus with clear-cut directives and goals, and your Pisces child will become a well-rounded human being.

Romance, love and marriage

Few people know how to love like Pisceans do. But your love is no ordinary love. And for this reason, 'raising the bar' five kilometres above ground is a big ask if you're looking for Mr or Mrs Right.

In your search for the perfect partner you will continually measure them against this incredibly unattainable standard. But that will probably only last a week and towards the end of that initial period of 'Oh my God, this is finally perfect!' you'll quickly realise you have made an error when putting your lover on a pedestal.

You see, Pisces aims at perfection and wants to see that perfection reflected back to them in others. However, you'll need to confront reality at some point, the truth that what you are dealing with in your romance is, after all, just another human being like yourself—warts and all.

You never allow romance to die. This is not the Piscean way. You're continually devising new ways to keep the flames of your passion burning, even into old age. You like to surprise your lover with shows of affection and novel techniques to demonstrate how you really feel for them.

Candlelit dinners, quiet moments together in natural settings, and even writing little notes expressing your love for them will be your way of letting them know that your love is true and for keeps. You're a sentimental individual. At the cinema, out of the corner of their eye, friends will occasionally observe you, shedding a quiet tear in the tragic parts of the film. Your lover should always have a spare handkerchief handy to help you wipe away your tears.

You'll give 150 per cent to each new affair of the heart, often wondering why you get back only 100 per cent. Why is it that, after all of your attempts to love others unconditionally, overlooking all of their faults, you will end up as the victim, the 'sacrificial lamb' on the altar of love? In all things—but most importantly in your relationships—try to look at life through a pair of real eyes. Take off those sepia-coloured sunglasses, Pisces, and you will see love as it really is.

If Pisces endures too many heartbreaks they may give up on love, opting to dwell in their favourite chair, self-medicating on chocolate and ice cream or, worse still, even on anti-depressants. A mid-life crisis might drive some Piscean wallflowers to go after a person who is unavailable; that is, someone who is married or downright wrong for them. Why? Well, in this case there'll be no possibility of being hurt again, will there?

Sex and intimacy are very important for Pisces. The physical expression of love is an extension of who you are and you're no less giving in these matters than in any other aspect of your love for a person. Venus and Libra are the planet and sign of relationships respectively and they dominate your zone of sexuality. Therefore, Pisces has a natural affinity with sex and physical intimacy. Once you meet the right person you can totally surrender yourself and truly understand the joys of wholesome lovemaking.

Choose your lovers carefully. Test them. Scrutinise their ways and ask others to validate your assessments. It sounds somewhat clinical but this is an essential screening process for a hopeless romantic like you. Once you meet your true soulmate, your heart will join with theirs and your efforts to please will be honestly returned.

With the right soulmate, marriage is the natural course for a true Piscean. This will ground you and give you the direction you so desperately desire. On top of that, marriage can give you the wonderful blessing of children. What could be more unconditional than loving and caring for your own kids?

Your caring ways will always be appreciated, but you should never give so much of yourself that you appear too needy. Never forget to love yourself as well. It's a good idea for you to develop independent activities in which you can expand yourself, separate from your relationships. Follow your romantic dreams, Pisces, but avoid nightmares where possible. You needn't be the victim when you have the chance of mastering your emotions and love.

Health, wellbeing and diet

Get the fundamentals right and you're well on your way to a physically viable life. And what are these fundamentals, you ask? 'Elementary, my dear Watson', replied Sherlock Holmes. They are: your emotions.

Pisces the water sign represents emotions, feelings and the astral component of human nature. The two fish that swim in opposite directions create an eddy of currents in the water of your emotional self, so this tumult must be dealt with first.

The way is simple: remain calm, meditate and relax. Chill out and feel content with this moment, the now. Stop wanting more. This will go a long way towards settling your mental and physical vibrations.

Hatha yoga or regular, flexible exercise are superb ways of strengthening all of these areas within you. It will make your muscles more supple, increase circulation and soothe your emotions. Generally, learning to relax and removing any self-defeating thought patterns will have a tonic effect on your mind and body.

Keeping to a regular regime of work, play, sleep and dietary habits will go a long way towards maintaining balanced health, both physically and emotionally. You tend to react so strongly to other people's emotions that it can affect your own mental wellbeing. Don't get too involved with the problems of others.

You should walk often but pay attention to your feet as well. Pisces-born folk may have problems in this area. Wear comfortable shoes and check if you need arch support.

A balanced diet must be added to the above regime. Never eat stale or 'bad' food. Always eat copious amounts of fruit and vegetables and opt for a low-lactose diet with adequate protein. This is an excellent Piscean path to health and wellbeing.

Vitamins A and B and magnesium are important for the long-term health of Pisces, so include broccoli, celery, green peppers, tomato, cherries, soybean products, bean sprouts, egg, and sunflower seeds in your diet.

To prevent weaknesses in your lower extremities, taking Vitamin B complex, plus beans and legumes, is a good idea. Reduce your fat intake because Pisces also relates to your liver. Consume foods that can help your digestion, and don't eat late at night.

Never, ever overeat, and always eat in a peaceful state of mind.

Work

You work best when helping others and solving their problems. This is an ingrained part of your nature. If you work solely for money, fame and power, you'll never feel quite fulfilled in your career.

You are emotional in your professional activities, but should contain this trait if you can. You tend to absorb the positive and negative emotions and vibrations of those in your environment, so pick your work colleagues carefully, if possible.

You may initially have difficulties choosing a clear-cut professional path due to your changeable mind. You're strongly motivated to pursue a career yet, at other times, have doubts as to what you would like to spend your life doing. You should research what you feel best suits your temperament.

You need to feel happy in your place of work to produce good things, but generally such careers as teaching, social work, welfare, medical and/or nursing fields would be ideal avenues of professional expression for you.

The television and film industry, as well as music and photographic design or any other artistic avenue will also satisfy your Piscean temperament.

Key to karma, spirituality and emotional balance

Your key words are 'I sacrifice' and therefore your challenge is to balance your desire to help and heal others with your own wellbeing. You live a life of surrender and love for others but must not become the sacrificial victim by giving away everything of yourself. Your intuition is very strong, so use it wisely.

I keep advising you to not become a victim, but your capacity to sacrifice yourself in order to help others is by far your greatest strength, even though at times it is your most challenging weakness. By all means approach life without too many expectations when you can, but also spend a little time pampering yourself through meditation, self-help and inner wisdom.

Use your intuition to help others and trust when inner messages tell you not to do something. You are in the last stage of your evolution and will experience many extraordinary things in your life.

Your lucky days

Your luckiest days are Mondays, Tuesdays, Thursdays and Sundays.

Your lucky numbers

Remember that the forecasts given later in the book will help you optimise your chances of winning. Your lucky numbers are:

9, 18, 27, 36, 45, 54, 63

2, 11, 20, 29, 38, 47, 56

7, 16, 25, 34, 43, 52, 61

Your destiny years

Your most important years are 7, 16, 25, 34, 43, 52, 61, 70, and 79.

Star Sign
Compatibility

Love and eggs are best when they are fresh.

—Russian Proverb

Romantic compatibility

How compatible are you with your current partner, lover or friend? Did you know that astrology can reveal a whole new level of understanding between people simply by looking at their star sign and that of their partner? In this chapter I'd like to share some special insights that will help you better appreciate your strengths and challenges using Sun sign compatibility.

The Sun reflects your drive, willpower and personality. The essential qualities of two star signs blend like two pure colours, producing an entirely new colour. Relationships, similarly, produce their own emotional colours when two people interact. The following is a general guide to your romantic prospects with others and how, by knowing the astrological 'colour' of each other, the art of love can help you create a masterpiece.

When reading the following I ask you to remember that no two star signs are ever *totally* incompatible. With effort and compromise, even the most 'difficult' astrological matches can work. Don't close your mind to the full range of life's possibilities! Learning about each other and ourselves is the most important facet of astrology.

Each star sign combination is followed by the elements of those star signs and the result of

Quick-reference guide: Horoscope compatibility between signs (percentage)

	Aries	Taurus	Gemini	Cancer	Leo	Virgo	Libra	Scorpio	Sagittarius	Capricorn	Aquarius	Pisces
Aries	60	70	65	65	90	45	70	80	90	50	55	65
Taurus	65	70	70	80	70	90	75	85	50	95	80	85
Gemini	65	70	75	60	80	75	90	60	75	50	90	50
Cancer	65	80	60	75	70	75	60	95	55	45	70	90
Leo	90	70	80	70	85	75	65	75	95	45	70	75
Virgo	45	90	75	75	75	70	80	85	70	95	50	70
Libra	70	75	90	60	65	80	80	85	80	85	95	50
Scorpio	80	85	60	95	75	85	85	90	85	65	60	95
Sagittarius	90	50	75	55	95	70	80	80	85	55	60	75
Capricorn	50	95	50	45	45	95	85	65	55	85	70	85
Aquarius	55	80	90	70	70	50	95	60	60	70	80	55
Pisces	65	85	50	90	75	70	50	95	75	85	55	80

their combining. For instance, Aries is a fire sign and Aquarius is an air sign and this combination produces a lot of 'hot air'. Air feeds fire and fire warms air. In fact, fire requires air. However, not all air and fire combinations work. I have included information about the different birth periods within each star sign and this will throw even more light on your prospects for a fulfilling love life with any star sign you choose.

Good luck in your search for love, and may the stars shine upon you in 2010!

Compatibility quick-reference guide

Each of the twelve star signs has a greater or lesser affinity with one another. The quick-reference guide will show you who's hot and who's not so hot as far as your relationships are concerned.

PISCES + ARIES
Water + Fire = Steam

If you decide to strike up a relationship with one of these hot-tempered rams, you'll soon realise the patience of Aries is always short lived. However, the combination of Pisces and Aries has its pros and cons, with your ruling planets of Neptune and Jupiter, and Aries' ruler Mars, being friendly in the planetary scheme of things.

There are difficulties trying to combine your energies with those of Aries. You will be challenged, that's for sure. Aries is direct, hot-tempered and very impatient. You work and live from a more emotional and spiritual base. This is why your elements of water and fire are also not particularly well suited. With your watery, emotional energy, Aries will feel dampened in spirit.

Aries does feel pleased by your compassionate sensitivity and this is the one thing that may keep them hanging around for a while. On the other hand, they are self-centred to a large extent—not all of them, but in general—and you might feel as if your needs are not always being met by this busy, frantic individual. Aries is a whirlwind of energy and, unless you're prepared to go with the flow, you might end up going it alone.

You like to communicate your feelings in ways that are not always verbal. You express your intuitive spiritual side using concepts that are far beyond the reach of most mortals, which is difficult for Aries to understand, the youngest of the zodiac signs. By this I mean that Pisces, being the most evolved of the star signs, won't feel as if Aries has the depth or breadth of understanding to accommodate its brand of living and lifestyle.

Aries is hot, that's why it is ruled by fire and, when it comes to sex, this is one of their primary domains of activity. They're abrupt, impatient and like to enjoy the physical side of love as much as possible. There can be some compatibility with them on this level, but you need more than the 'Wham, bam, thank you ma'am' kind of scenario, which is what some of the less-sensitive Aries are like. You'll have your work cut out for you, teaching them the art of lovemaking and intimacy from an emotional and spiritual vantage point.

However, there are three grades of Aries, so we shouldn't jump to conclusions. Those born between the 21st and the 30th of March are extremely passionate and to a large extent are responsive in love, but they can also be erratic and inconsistent in their communication. Mars, the planet which doubly dominates these individuals, means that they have well-developed egos and will often not listen to other people's opinions. That's a stumbling block, isn't it?

Because your star sign falls in the twelfth zone to Aries, this can complicate relationships with those born between the 31st of March and the 10th of April. Such things as your health and vitality, debts and other work-related issues will be a point of contention and the two of you will not always agree.

Aries born between the 11th and the 20th of April are quite fiery and motivated individuals, but they also like lots of change. Unless you're prepared to bend with the wind, you might find life a little difficult with them. One saving grace is their sensitive and loving nature, which resonates with yours.

PISCES + TAURUS
Water + Earth = Mud

Taurus, like Pisces, is feminine in nature and therefore you'll experience a high degree of mutual sensitivity together. This is reflected in your planets, Neptune and Jupiter and also Venus, which rules Taurus.

This sensitivity extends to artistic creativity, sensual and sexual interplay. Through their personality, Taurus also adds a much greater level of practicality to your relationship, which should work well for you, given that you are sometimes 'off with the fairies', aren't you, Pisces?

You have a receptiveness and natural attraction towards Taurus, liking their need for security and their uncanny ability to be resourceful with money and the things of this world. Conversely, although they are rather earthy individuals, they see the benefits you bring to the table with your deep insights and sensitive, compassionate and universal outlook. In other words, such two extremes can balance each other quite well in this match.

Because you live in a world of ideas—or should I say, a world of fantasy—Taurus will want you to be just a little bit more practical, so you need to focus more on what they're saying or Taurus will become rather exasperated with your lack of concentration. If you manage to do this, as difficult as the discipline may sound, it will improve your relationship with Taurus and you'll be more than satisfied with the long-term benefits it will provide both of you.

Pisces and Taurus have a different way of communicating as well, so you must be clear and concise in the way you express your ideas or Taurus will get frustrated and sometimes angry. They are very unambiguous in their communication style, being rather black and white in pretty much everything they say and do.

You mustn't talk in Zen Buddhist riddles but try to fulfil their practical requirements by giving them your perspective on things. Taurus, as we've already said, is primarily concerned with security but with a patient and creative bull, the two of you can utilise your spiritual and imaginative personality to create something wonderful, even in a business sense. Work together should be something that you consider as a unit.

Friendship, love and married life is more than likely going to be an exciting journey for you and Taureans born between the 21st and the 29th of April. These individuals will ground you and therefore you can expect a durable love affair with them. These Taureans, like most of them, are loyal, appreciate beauty, and have a deep affinity with family.

With Taureans born between the 30th of April and the 10th of May, you can also feel satisfied that any commitment given by them, particularly when it comes to marriage, will be for the long haul. They are also very sensual and passionate individuals so your intimate connection with them is also something that can be relied upon.

The one class of Taureans with whom you might not be quite so fulfilled is those born between the 11th and the 21st of May. They are a more serious class of Taureans, being ruled by Saturn and Capricorn, which makes them practical but not particularly responsive in the bedroom.

PISCES + GEMINI
Water + Air = Rain

If you pointed out to most Geminis that they are rather flighty, scattered and diverse in their thinking processes, they'd probably simply smile, agree with you and, in a strange sort of way, feel quite complimented by your observations. And you, Pisces, understand that your inner psychic rovings sometimes make you appear out of touch with the world around you. So is there any wonder that a Pisces and Gemini coming together is a rather unusual match, in that there doesn't seem to be too much anchoring either of you to Mother Earth?

However, you're both keen to explore mental and emotional realms and this will bring you together through mutual love and respect. The two of you fall under the category of being mutable signs, which make you changeable and hard to pin down; but at the same time, flexible and adaptable both to the environment and people surrounding you. You're able to adjust at those times when it is necessary.

The one big drawback is that you are scattered individuals with so many diverse interests that it begs the question as to whether or not you have time to dedicate yourselves to the long path of commitment in love. The two of you are hell-bent on exploring life in all its variety of colours. Therefore, a lifestyle of spontaneous change, travel and movement doesn't exactly lend itself to a family existence, does it?

Gemini is primarily motivated by thought processes and the spoken word, which is indicated by their ruling element of air and its planet Mercury. You, Pisces, being ruled by water, operate from the gut level, from what you feel rather than what you think. Although you are great friends, these two diverse approaches to the way you live your lives and how you express your feelings could be a sticking point in the relationship.

Gemini is receptive to your many nuances but they probably talk a little too much for your liking. You'd just love Gemini to understand that silence is probably the most eloquent form of speech, but that may not happen in this lifetime, so you'll just have to put up with a little bit of chit-chat now and then.

As with all of the star signs, there are different classes within the one zodiac group. Geminis born between the 22nd of May and the 1st of June are true Geminis in every sense of the word and have great minds but like to live in an impulsive and exciting way. Understanding them will be difficult because it's hard to tie them down.

If the birthday of your Gemini partner falls between the 2nd and the 12th of June, you can enjoy great friendship with them and you'll be fulfilled romantically and sexually, but there could be that one little thing missing. What is it, I wonder?

Finally, teaming up with a Gemini born between the 13th and the 21st of June will be a rather hit-and-miss affair. Their spontaneity will unsettle you, but nonetheless you'll still enjoy each other's company. Let me say again that this group of Geminis is not exactly the crème de la crème of marriage choices for Pisces.

PISCES + CANCER
Water + Water = Deluge

You don't have to go much further than Cancer to find your almost perfect soulmate. The reason for this is that both of you fall under the category of the water element, which means your personalities match each other very well due to your warmth, sensitivity and caring natures.

When your elements are the same, there is a subconscious synchronicity and an unspoken understanding that seems to hint at some deeper karmic fulfilment through your coming together.

Cancer, like you, Pisces, is one of the most empathetic signs of the zodiac and you'll imme-diately relate to the way they go about their daily business. They are selfless people to a large extent, like yourself, and have the ability to return the affec-tion and demonstrativeness that you so much love to give in your relationships.

You both live in the realm of feelings. Yes, this is a positive personality trait, but taken to the extreme it can be rather difficult for both of you to deal with, especially when we see just how much your feelings oscillate. Each of you in turn can be moody, which could take up huge slabs of time to resolve if you're choosing a serious life path together. You are both hypersensitive to your surroundings and probably more so to each other. A bit of leeway is what's needed to balance the heart of this relationship.

Cancer accepts your views and philosophical perceptions. They won't at all dismiss your intuitive responses to life and will in fact support you 100 per cent. They too have the uncanny ability to sense what's actually going on around them and, when you bring these two very developed intuitive powers to the relationship, most of the time you won't need to say too much to understand each other.

You are touchy, feely people, but Cancer can at times be a little less open and sometimes holds grudges. You have the ability to take them beyond these self-limiting emotions and, therefore, the final outcome of this relationship is one in which you both understand the true meaning of love. The Pisces–Cancer match is one of the few soulmate combinations in the zodiac that can work for you.

If born between the 22nd of June and the 3rd of July, this Cancerian partner will be extremely emotional, perhaps way too much for you to deal with. Coupled with your pendulous moods, the two of you will find little substance to anchor your feelings. This is a relationship of many strong reactions between the two of you.

An excellent match can be expected with Cancerians born between the 4th and the 13th of July. You have a tremendous two-way line of communication, which is full of compassion and love. On your deepest level, you'll feel connected, fulfilled and more than happy to consider marriage with them.

Your connections with Cancerians born between the 14th and the 23rd of July are also very strong. You feel secure and comforted in your friendship with them and you encourage each other to develop the relationship over time and not let it get stale.

PISCES + LEO

Water + Fire = Steam

Leo-born people are very proud individuals, so most people might be forgiven for mistaking them as egotistical, self-serving individuals. However, that's not really the case and fortunately your inbuilt Pisces intuition will tell you this.

Leo's warmth and dramatic energy is intoxicating, not just to you but to anyone who comes in contact with them. You will find yourself competing for their attention and, if you're not strong in asserting yourself some of the time, you may just fall by the wayside while they endeavour to explore their lives with their intense sense of adventure.

Leo loves the fact that you are sensitive, romantic and loving to them. But it is starting to sound like it's all about them, isn't it? Not really. Leo won't be able to resist your lovingness and this will encourage you, giving you the confidence to stay a little longer to see where this relationship might end up. The bottom line is that you'll both have to make sacrifices, compromise and concede that you're human and no relationship is going to be 100 per cent fulfilling all of the time.

Leo wants you to be more self-confident and they're happy to help you overcome some of these weaknesses, particularly in a social arena, if you're somewhat withdrawn. But they must understand that this has to happen in your own good time. If you feel pushed, this will result in you being emotionally threatened and it just won't work.

You have an unusual sexual connection with Leo, and because Jupiter is one of your ruling planets and is also a lucky planet for Leo, it's quite likely there will be some subtle elements of your passionate interactions that keep the flame of love alive. If you're both prepared to enter this relationship with a sense of adventure and understanding of both yourselves and each other, then the partnership could even become a little addictive.

Your sense of self-sacrifice will be tested if you enter into a relationship with a Leo born between the 24th of July and the 4th of August. These Leo-born characters want so much of your energy that it might be hard for you to feel as if you can sustain such high levels of drive and passion. Your watery element might extinguish the fire of their passion.

With Leos born between the 5th and the 14th of August, there's also a very natural attraction because of the karmic influence of Sagittarius on these individuals. There's a natural sort of comfort from being with each other and there is also a high degree of sexual attraction thrown in for good measure.

Passion also seems to be the name of the game in your attachment with any Leo born between the 15th and the 23rd of August. Fiery and sexy Mars will drive these people and quite likely stimulate your passion as well.

PISCES + VIRGO
Water + Earth = Mud

You, Pisces, see life through your spiritual and intuitive aspirations, whereas Virgo is a highly intellectual character. Your perspectives on life differ dramatically, but this is not to say you can't find some convergence through a deeper understanding of each other's opinions.

In an unusual type of similarity, you are both primarily motivated by the idea of serving and helping others. Virgos are perfectionists, however, and they show this by continuously using a very analytical process that you find not just impossible to grasp, but also distasteful. Your emotions don't appreciate the intellectual, deductive approach of Virgo.

And speaking of perfection, Virgos are nitpickers for improving things, for making things more efficient. Therefore, in your estimation, they don't like to accept anything as it is. That's where you'll both have some problems, too. I'm not saying you don't want to improve either yourself or things you know aren't working well, but you also like the simple idea of acceptance and to a large extent the philosophy of surrendering to the flow of life. These are very different life views, so to make this relationship work, even though you are opposite signs of the zodiac, means you'll really have to work hard at it.

Considerable changeability and emotional fluctuation in both your personalities will test you but also keep your daily lifestyles quite interesting. If you can accept each other as human beings with inbuilt faults then your support for each other will be coming from the heart, the right space within you, and this is all you need to propel your relationship forward in the most positive way. Don't try to change but accept each other as you are and, if you need to do any changing, make sure you're working on yourself first. That's the secret to the Pisces–Virgo match.

Sexually, you probably feel a little funny dealing with Virgo. You get the sense that their lovemaking and emotional expression is rather contrived and premeditated. You'd prefer to see a lot more spontaneity, creativity and genuine heart-to-heart connectivity. That may be something that is not going to fulfil you in this relationship.

A match with a Virgo born between the 24th of August and the 2nd of September will not fare too badly and perhaps destiny does have something special lined up for you. Expressing emotions from your heart will soften Virgo's intellectual temperament and your intimacy together will also be satisfying. Being opposite signs, marriage is also not out of the question.

Financial prospects for you and a Virgo born between the 3rd and 12th of September are quite good. Generally they have a good compatibility rating with you, but this is more a practical affair rather than one of great passion.

A romantic liaison with Virgos born between the 13th and the 23rd of September is a hit-and-miss affair. You'll both be tested in your ability to sacrifice for each other and may never quite feel fulfilled by your opposite sign of Virgo.

PISCES + LIBRA
Water + Air = Rain

Librans are born under the sign of air, indicating their love of people, social activities and spontaneous, creative, changeable personalities.

This doesn't bother you too much and can in fact stimulate you, if not challenge you, to become better in the social arena, arm in arm with your Libran counterpart. It's when the Libran becomes a little too flirtatious that you feel as if the sanctity of your relationship is being violated. Libra will never feel this is the case, but you, being the idealist in love, have a different opinion.

Pisceans too can flirt and do desire to attract the attention of potential partners, but Librans are the masters of this and you'll never be able to one-up them. Therefore you could continue to feel as if you're 'getting the short end of the stick' in a love affair with them.

Once you become comfortable with your Libran lover you'll feel sexually compatible and the reason for this is that the ruler of Libra, Venus, gains great strength from its placement in your Sun sign of Pisces. It reaches extraordinary heights, which would make Libra feel uplifted and emotionally and sexually fulfilled. There is therefore something going for this relationship.

Librans are chatterboxes, or at least many of them are. You don't necessarily feel that this constant stream of words is necessary to communicate ideas or, more importantly, feelings. If only you could get them on the same page as you on this point. Patience, Pisces.

You'll both be forced to grow spiritually in spite of yourselves in a relationship together. Your personal, social and sexual spheres of understanding will expand dramatically. The two of you need to talk about this or rather, should I say, simply sit and be with each other, to experience expansion in each other's company.

Venus is a strong in Pisces and will therefore bring you great satisfaction with Librans born between the 24th of September and the 4th of October. You should endeavour to put aside your differences and really give this relationship a go because marriage is quite likely on the cards with them, even if you do vary in some of the ways you view life.

Librans born between the 5th and the 13th of October are fast, progressive thinkers with very powerful personalities. You can't quite figure out what their next moves are going to be and this can be rather unsettling to you. Tradition is a key ingredient for the Piscean to feel comfortable and, unfortunately, these Librans are not exactly masters of commitment, at least not in the first part of their lives.

A relationship with any Libran born between the 14th and the 23rd of October is very positive and I can confidently say you'll feel wonderfully stimulated in their company. You can expect oodles of growth and many new friends and chances to travel in your joining of hands with them. These Librans do have the flirting bug, but your stabilising influence on them may eventually draw a commitment from them if you persist.

PISCES + SCORPIO
Water + Water = Deluge

Yet again, the water–water combination of Pisces and Scorpio is an almost flawless match, indicating a deep soulmateship of the finest level. This would have to be one of the best combinations of zodiac signs.

You may feel as if you've hit the jackpot once you set eyes on your powerful and magnetic Scorpio friend. There's no doubt that your destinies were meant to intertwine and this will be evident immediately on meeting them. If instantaneous and intuitive communication is what you're looking for, Scorpio is the ideal partner with whom to achieve this. They will know just what you're feeling and can even telepathically convey their intentions to you. You absolutely love this.

Because you have such an innate understanding of each other's needs, you have no problem serving each other and in fully supplying those requirements that are the foundation of the most loving of relationships.

You both have an intuitive understanding of what the other is thinking or needs, and without question or discussion, will promptly be there for them. This almost magical communication between you will sustain the relationship for a long time to come. And, as with many Pisces–Scorpio relationships, even if you do for some reason run into snags and need to break it off for a while, the power of attraction is too strong for you not to give it another go.

You'll be dealing with the most intense of zodiac signs but you, more than any other, know how to cushion that impact and make it work to your benefit. Scorpio also realises you've surrendered completely in this match and they don't doubt your love. Remember, they are also very possessive, jealous individuals, and the selfless love you offer them is an endorsement of your loyalty, which will keep them attached to you forever.

Scorpios born between the 24th of October and the 2nd of November have a magnetic attraction to you. It doesn't matter how long you stay with these people, your life will be transformed by your contact with them. This is a soul-stirring combination.

There's also a very powerful attraction with Scorpios born between the 3rd and the 12th of November. This relationship flows very easily and your staunch loyalty to each other will become the bedrock of a lasting union.

You'll find a powerful soulmate in a Scorpio born between the 13th and the 22nd of November. They are sensitive and even somewhat reactive like yourself, but there is still a very high level of compatibility between you. Your life will be exciting with them and if you want something more than the typical day-by-day routine lifestyle, this Scorpio is the one for you.

PISCES + SAGITTARIUS
Water + Fire = Steam

The fact that Pisces and Sagittarius are ruled by similar planets means there are inherent similarities you both identify with on meeting each other. You admire the Sagittarian's love of life, their reverence for things, and the expansive optimism they exude. And you, with Neptune also ruling you alongside Jupiter, have both psychic and spiritual wisdom they also respect.

Sagittarius wants to learn about the dreamy, compassionate and intuitive facets of your character. You are in a sense a spiritual teacher for them; whereas it is equally true they have also come to teach you many things about the world and how to enjoy your life a little bit more than you might have done so far.

Sagittarius is a fire sign, which reflects their spontaneous, creative and generous personalities. It's pretty hard not to love a Sagittarian, even if at times their words are a little blunt and can inflict wounds on your sensitive Piscean emotions. You're a forgiving type of individual, so you'll usually understand that when Sagittarius 'shoots from the hip', it's not an intentional dig at you and you can let their comments slide.

Sagittarians are rolling stones that gather no moss, being lovers of travel, so this may not augur well for a domestic existence if family life is what you want. Giving them the opportunity to expend their energy, sow their wild oats and see the world may mean you will have to wait just a little bit longer until they return to you and decide they want to settle down. That's not a bad idea if there's any hope of you maintaining a long-term relationship with your Sagittarian counterpart.

Sagittarius makes you both generous, especially in the bedroom, so your sexual contact should be quite good. Sagittarians are excessive, particularly in their love of pleasure and ease of living. You need to ramp up your energy levels to maintain their pace between the sheets.

There's one group of Sagittarians born between the 23rd of November and the 1st of December who will really relate well to you. You'll feel compatible with these individuals and vice versa.

There's also a good sense of love and camaraderie with those born between the 2nd and 11th of December, but bear in mind they are individuals who can get angry at the drop of a hat and their straight-shooting communication may persistently hurt you.

There are problems in your communication with Sagittarians born between the 12th and 22nd of December, so you need to lay down the ground rules before going too far with them. Talk clearly and concisely about what you want and don't be afraid to ask them what their spin on love and marriage is as well.

PISCES + CAPRICORN
Water + Earth = Mud

Saturn rules Capricorn-born individuals, therefore you'll need to expect them to move much more slowly than other star signs such as Aries or Scorpio. Even friendships may not go to plan because you're constantly wondering what they may be thinking or what their intentions are. Capricorns find it hard to trust others until many experiences have been gained from their contact with you. This requires immense patience on your part, Pisces.

You mustn't make the mistake of feeling that the solemn and sometimes stern demeanour of Capricorn is a reaction to you. This is just the way they are, particularly younger Capricorns. Believe it or not, they do lighten up quite a bit as they get older, which is a rather unusual astrological personality trait.

Like the other earth signs of Taurus and Virgo, Capricorn is practical and sometimes overly so, being caught up in the idea that who they are must always be measured by what they have.

This is diametrically opposed to the Piscean ideal, in that who you are has nothing much to do with what you own or how much money you're able to earn, but rather how much you're able to give, how much you're able to sacrifice and how, in the process of sharing your love, you're able to uplift others less fortunate than yourself. Finding a common meeting ground will be difficult because your life philosophies are truly quite different.

You're sexually attracted to each other, but there is a somewhat inhibiting energy bound up in this combination. Dealing with the stern and some-times icy-cold exterior of Capricorn will require your warmest, most tender advances to help open them up.

You get on extremely well with Capricorns born between the 23rd of December and the 1st of

January. There's a great understanding you'll share and that understanding will become the bedrock of a really good relationship if you choose it to be. These Capricorns will not be the blistering, fiery and sexy Arians or Scorpios we've talked about, but they do offer you a quiet, stable security, which is also important to you.

You're loyally supported by Capricorns born between the 2nd and the 10th of January. They lead highly organised lives and may not be as spontaneous as you desire, but they are affectionate in their own way and you may not be able to refuse the financial and material benefits that go with a relationship with them.

A Capricorn born between the 11th and the 20th of January is a good potential marriage partner for you. This is because Virgo and its ruling planet Mercury do have a large part to play in their lives. This sign of the zodiac, as we mentioned earlier with the Virgo readings, is your marriage sign and so there's a strong sense of having met your soulmate with them. They are not the greatest match for you but it is certainly one that can work and over time offer you tremendous fulfilment.

PISCES + AQUARIUS
Water + Air = Rain

Pisces and Aquarius are called 'impersonal' signs of the zodiac, which means there's a greater cause to which you are both drawn. You have common interests, with you trying hard to uplift those less fortunate than yourself, and with Aquarius mindful of the social changes that are necessary to create a better world for everyone. So in this sense your ideals, generally speaking, can be quite similar.

Aquarius is an air sign so they have a somewhat intellectual leaning, are very studious and can often be rather fixed in their opinions. They need someone like you, Pisces, to show them that you can still maintain an opinion but exercise flexibility to gain greater and higher insights as one gets older.

Secrets are a part of the Pisces–Aquarius match because Aquarius is the sign of hidden involvement, past karma and clandestine events to Pisces. This could be the case with you and your Aquarian partner. You may meet in the most bizarre way and could even have to suppress the nature of your relationship for a while due to social, religious or other cultural constraints.

Stability may not be a strong enough point in this relationship and therefore you'll have to find other positive attributes to which you can both hitch your dreams.

On a positive note, your imagination and their broader view of the world blend well to produce a most fascinating romantic relationship. Although you don't think exactly the same way, your communication can provide you both a whole new gamut of information and ideas from which you can draw strength and creative aspiration.

Your sexual relationship is also quite powerful due to the Aquarian desire to explore and experiment sexually. Your sensitivity, combined with their progressive and avant-garde tastes, is certainly something you wouldn't want to miss out on, even if it is simply to have an experience you'll want to remember at some time in the future.

Your connections with Aquarians born between the 21st and the 30th of January can be full of confusions and ambiguities. This is a hot–cold, on–off type of relationship that could drive you nuts over time. You need to have clear parameters by which to engage each other.

Aquarians born between the 31st of January and the 8th of February are busy individuals and may not have any time to give to you. You might think that's a shame until you realise they're quite flighty, free and individual characters who don't really have as much to offer you as you would like.

Aquarians born between the 9th and 19th of February are also rather interesting characters who attract you. They are sensitive like you and also enjoy the company of others. Libra and its ruling planet Venus have a strong connection with them, and it is also a lucky planet for you, so by all means explore this relationship because it may offer you some interesting twists and turns.

PISCES + PISCES
Water + Water = Deluge

It's not always easy for star twins to generate enough staying power in a relationship because they are just so similar to each other. In your case, teaming up with another Pisces, adding water to water, elementally could create a teary affair, to say the least.

There's an abundance of emotion, perhaps way too much emotion, to make this a practical enough relationship to go the full distance. Your changing and complex moods will need to be managed individually and jointly for you to get this relationship off the ground.

Try encouraging each other to get more organised and practical. Being the dreamy types that you are, the worst thing you could do is be hung up in the clouds at a time when things are falling apart down here on Earth. Remember, you can't simply disappear and leave behind a dirty backyard.

Your love for your Pisces partner will be true and in the same way they will extend their deepest feelings to you as well. Only you both know just how idealistic and true your love is for each other. But that's not enough. To make this a permanent and fulfilling relationship, it has to be balanced by many other factors. Ignoring this would be disastrous for a Pisces–Pisces team.

You're both preoccupied with assisting others, most notably your own families. Getting caught up in the problems and the dilemmas of other relatives is counteractive to the cause of your love for each other. Draw a line in the sand; understand that, if you want this relationship to work, your relationship has to be number one. This doesn't in any way mean, however, that you can't continue in your compassionate roles in your families and society at large.

With other Pisceans born between the 20th and the 28th or 29th February, you share the vision of love and can encourage each other to achieve a more selfless spiritual state. You are both on the path of self-realisation and often enjoy a cloistered environment in which you can share each other's love without anyone else encroaching on your time together.

With Pisces born between the 1st and the 10th of March, your home life will be important to you. You will both nurture each other and be loyal parents, enjoying the conventions of family life and society generally. You're both a little changeable in mood and this may need to be sorted out to improve the relationship.

If you get entangled with another Piscean born between the 11th and the 20th of March, bear in mind that Scorpio and Pluto have a hand in their destinies and make them very intense, passionate types. They are jealous and also demand a lot more of you than you may be prepared to give. If you are indeed a more submissive type of personality, you'll be able to handle the domineering, passionate and sexual personalities of those born in this period. Your destinies together are also quite strong.

2010:
The Year Ahead

Flow with whatever is happening and let your mind be free. Stay centred by accepting whatever you are doing. This is the ultimate.

—Chuang Tzu

Romance and friendship

You will have undergone significant changes and adjustments in your romantic life or marriage throughout 2009, so you may well be dusting yourself off and asking the question: 'What exactly is going to happen romantically for me in 2010?' The answer requires you to put aside your emotion for a moment to get to the bottom of why things are happening.

Both Saturn and Mars surround your zone of marriage, which indicates continued frustration and the likely desire to find some sort of escape route through your closest friends and social allies. You are known for your idealism and, although this may seem like the perfect exit strategy, it may only work for a while and then you'll be left dealing with the same old issues.

Fortunately the lunar eclipse on the 1st of January, which occurs in your zone of romance, creativity and love affairs, shows clearly that many deep and significant insights will be realised and you'll have the perfect opportunity to make some sense of what's been happening with your spouse or partner.

In January and February your social affairs are spotlighted, with Jupiter also expanding your popularity and self-confidence after the 18th. Throughout the first two months of the year, however, you may have a tendency to overdo things, to push yourself to the limits and possibly even ingratiate yourself by trying to make yourself out to be something you are not. The secret of popularity and success in friendship—and in anything, for that matter—is simply to be yourself.

Weight and diet issues might also be of concern to you, especially in the early part of 2010. Pay special attention to your diet, lifestyle and other aspects such as your attitude, all of which have an important bearing not only upon how you feel but how you look. Unfortunately people can judge you by how you appear, rather than by who you are.

When Venus conjoins Uranus in March, you can expect an exciting period to commence in your life. You're probably asking: 'But what about all those other difficult challenges you mentioned at the outset of my 2010 reading?' Well, of course these are the underlying challenges of your life, but they're not going to stop you from having fun, meeting people, developing your skills in communication and even making love.

Throughout March and April you will be keen to extend your circle of influence and connect with others who are a little different to your usual peer group. You may be impulsive at this time, so make sure your mind balances your emotional charges.

Communication will be fundamental to your satisfaction, particularly in April and May. With Venus transiting your third zone of communications and also in a powerful aspect to Pluto, you'll be more likely to speak your mind rather than mulling over your feelings and bottling up these expressions.

You will feel somewhat out of sorts throughout May, particularly up until the 19th, when your self-image wavers. As I said earlier, you must be yourself and not try to assume a role or persona that is completely out of touch with who you are. You may have fantasies and ideals that have been long suppressed and might try strategies to continue to sweep these feelings under the rug. Keep in mind it's best to be true to yourself and experience what you have to.

Avoiding your karma, a soulmate or someone for whom you have strong feelings will be almost impossible after the 20th May, when Venus enters your zone of love. You may be torn between showing your feelings and holding back, which may also be due to the concurrent Jupiter–Saturn interplay. Should you give in to your feelings, or should you hold back? This will be one of the primary issues causing confusion and also impacting upon your self-identity and ego. You may be more concerned with what others think of you rather than doing what your heart tells you is the right thing for your happiness.

Venus will oppose Pluto at this time, so love affairs and feelings can become intense, almost unbearable, and possibly even obsessive. You will need to find an adequate outlet, a healthy avenue of expression, otherwise this could lead to physical illness as a result of suppressing your emotions for too long.

Throughout June sudden events change the status quo of your family. Dealing with those who are not handling life well will require you to be there for them. Spending money on noble causes will require sacrifices, for which you are well known, because yours is the most sacrificial sign of the twelve zodiac tribes.

During June your love, expenses and the condition of a loved one or friend may be intimately linked. You may need to give of your time, money or additional affection to help someone deal with some personal problems, a loss or, heaven forbid, a personal tragedy.

A new understanding can be reached throughout the middle of the year and this will be heralded by the lunar eclipse in your zone of friendships. I can foresee you extending your reach as a personality, making friends with those near and far, and working more passionately to attract people who will reciprocate the same level of love and compassion that you offer others.

Wonderful results can be expected at this time due to the important connections that the planet of love Venus makes with some of the other planets. Marriage, long-term commitment and the more traditional values that society upholds will be uppermost in your mind. Making such a commitment will be highlighted very strongly throughout July. Not only that, an additional power point, a solar eclipse, which is affecting your love affairs, could well indicate for those of marriageable age that this is the time to 'dive in, boots 'n' all'!

However, your idealism will be out of touch with reality as Venus moves into a challenging aspect to Neptune. You might not want to listen to what others have to say about your decisions and perhaps even your behaviour. You will try to buck the system, become angry and turn your back on those who actually offer you valuable advice. Clarity and earnestness should be your weapons against problems of all sorts.

Mars and Jupiter are in a powerful aspect throughout August, indicating a strong need for sexual contact. At the same time Saturn will be putting the brakes on someone else's expression. There will be a lopsided amount of affection and demonstrativeness on your part, with little satisfaction in return. Your altruistic view of love and selfless giving will most certainly be challenged throughout August and September. But you mustn't let a little bump in the road of life cause you to withdraw the love you possess in such abundance.

Perhaps a journey, some time out, will be necessary throughout September. Your ruling planet is in fact Neptune and its travel through the zone of emigration and long-distant journeys prods you to investigate those deeper spiritual yearnings through unusual avenues. Meditation, Tantra, qigong and philosophies that unravel the mysteries of life will curiously attract you under these planetary transits. And you may well meet someone who either triggers these interests or is totally in sync with you. This is a time frame in which soulmates may also come out of the woodwork and instant connections with friends can be made.

You are more certain of your place in life when Mars moves to the upper part of your horoscope in late October. Throughout November you will be keen to exert your influence on the world and will feel a surge of super-confidence making your personality felt wherever you go. You are not the sort of person to dominate and coerce others unfairly, so this will be a welcome injection of positive energy that helps you persuade others in a wonderfully natural and convincing way to give you the things in life that you know you deserve. This should be a very satisfying feeling and incidentally is a transit that will bring you much respect.

Mars continues to bring with it many blessings personally and socially throughout November and December. In December, when it connects with your zone of friendship, personal life ideals, siblings and profitability, you can expect this final stage of 2010 to be full of life, vitality and exciting social opportunities. There are, however, a few negative implications in that arguments will arise due to your animated style. You will not be prepared to accept anything at face value or what others are trying to shove down your throat, even if they are fully convinced it is the best thing for you.

You will feel independent, enlightened and capable of making decisions for yourself. The year 2010 looks like it will be a year in which the many lessons you have learned, the many experiences that have come your way, can only serve to make you a much better person who is fulfilled in your friendships and love affairs.

Work and money

Your work, ambition and finance planets are Jupiter, the Sun, Mars and Saturn. Throughout 2010 Jupiter will assume an even greater role in your affairs as it moves into your Sun sign in January.

Work will take on an increasing importance and you will tend to be identified with what you do. As the powerful and expansive, yet benevolent, energies of this planet begin to swell, success is likely to come to you in ways that you could have hardly imagined.

You will be conscious of your abilities and have a strong yearning to expand your understanding, develop your skills and earn more money, even if global trends dictate that this seems impossible. For you, in 2010, anything is possible!

Initially you might not have the support of others due to Saturn and Mars surrounding your public relations zone. This shows others are reluctant to part with their money, partner up with you in your projects, and will generally be slow off the mark in making their feelings and intentions known.

In March, however, Venus is well poised to bring you some profits and increased earnings after the 7th. Its fine aspect with Mars means that the dynamic planet ruling your zone of fortune and finance will bring you additional benefits, bonuses and the gift of the gab.

I mentioned in your romance section that when Venus moved into your zone of communications, your relationships would improve. Well, we can extend this aspect to your professional activities as well, especially if negotiations are part and parcel of your day-to-day routine. Contracts and other forms of agreement will flow much more smoothly and even customers and business partners who are usually a little reluctant to give you a firm decision quickly, will be easily persuaded by you throughout this time frame.

Throughout March, April and May there are wonderful opportunities in your professional life and you must be prepared to investigate them. I always say the worst thing that can happen to a human being is for them to be lying on their death bed at the end of lives, wishing they had tried something out. It will be too late then. What's the worst that can happen? Have no fear and take a punt, just to see where it takes you.

You may find some opposition from those in your workplace or your employer throughout May. That may last for a couple of weeks up until the

26th, when Venus once again comes to the rescue and provides ample positive and popular energy, giving you the chance to overturn bad decisions made by others. During this phase as well, Uranus will bring with it some unexpected financial or premier opportunities.

In June and July your ideals and perhaps even your career direction may change for the better. The eclipse in your zone of life fulfilment and profit is a good indicator that you will have armed yourself with some new and powerful information that makes you confident enough to step out of the shadows and into the light of your true path. You should take up any new offer that gives you the chance to earn more money, accept a new position or generally exert your power over others.

July and August are significant in that savings and future security will be a focus of your attention. You often operate from the level of intuition. Unfortunately the advice you receive may be so intellectual at this time that it goes against the grain of your gut feeling. This will be a dilemma and once again the best course of action is to balance the facts with what your heart tells you is the correct decision.

When negotiating with bankers, financiers and others who seem to know more than you, remember that many huge multinational conglomerates, banks and other institutions have fallen to the ground like a house of cards, so 'expertise' doesn't always necessarily guarantee the best outcome. Your gut feelings will probably be correct.

In the last part of the year, try not to get bogged down in cold comfort. You will feel as though your routine is adequate but your inner heart and ambitious drive this year will want you to look further afield. With Venus in the ninth zone of foreign culture, travel and higher education, these last few weeks of the year will beckon you to investigate other opportunities that will take you well beyond your previous conditioning. This is an excellent end to the year in that it gives you the confidence to try new things and beckons you into 2011 and beyond.

Karma, luck and meditation

One's future karma is shown by the fifth zone of the zodiac or horoscope. In your case there is a lunar eclipse in the first month of the year, indicating a very serious consideration of your future and what lies in store for you. I can tell you immediately that Jupiter's entrance into your Sun sign for the first time in twelve years in the latter part of January will usher in a brand new period of hope, insight and luck for most Pisceans.

You are spiritually activated throughout June, July and August, but you must also be careful, particularly if you are a younger Piscean in your teens or early twenties and have the opportunity to experiment with narcotics, alcohol or illegal forms of mind-altering substances.

These will certainly give you an expanded state of consciousness—temporarily—but the comedown will be heavy. You could be curious to find out about your true nature and the real meaning of happiness and peace. By far the better path is meditation, a clean lifestyle and introverted self-analysis.

I said earlier that, in your romantic twelfth house, many new insights would come your way this year and my intuition tells me that these insights will have a lasting impact upon your life all round. In September, Venus in fine aspect to Neptune from your zone of past karma, and Mars also entering your zone of past karma, will bring you an under-standing of, and in many cases resolutions to, your past conflicts, family difficulties and unresolved emotional complexes.

These are the psychological backbone of many problems we confront in life. What a wonderful thing that you have the opportunity through the blessings of Jupiter to feel good about yourself, to let go of those past grievances or grudges. You can make amends with family members, relatives and other friends and find peace within yourself.

Towards the end of the year, if you are able to lift your awareness to these refreshing new heights, your energies will shine and you will be poised to attract a whole new set of circumstances, people and wonderful good fortune in your life.

Let the stars shine upon you and bring you the best for 2010, Pisces!

2010:
Month By Month
Predictions

Control your destiny or somebody else will.

—Jack Welch

Highlights of the month

January goes off with a bang as the lunar eclipse stimulates your romantic and creative pleasures. From the 1st till the 7th, you'll be in fine form and have ample opportunity to express your deepest feelings and enjoy the company of those who truly appreciate you.

Most of your attention in the first week of the month will definitely be on connecting more deeply with your spouse or partner and they too will enjoy your company. Try to steady your affections after the 8th, however, because you may be demanding a little more than others can offer you. This could cause you to feel a little down and you could start to view life and relationships as somewhat of a paradox.

You can redirect your feelings in a positive fashion after the 13th and with no less than five planets occupying your zone of social activity you will be surrounded by friends in some very engaging environments. But during this same period, you may feel overly intense in your feelings and could start to alienate others.

You need to back off when an issue of something private, or perhaps a secret, is raised and you push a little too hard to demand someone reveals this information. Extracting the truth can sometimes be a shocking pleasure! If they do reveal their deepest feelings, it will be a paltry, nervous victory for you.

Health matters are spotlighted from the 20th. You are probably overdoing things a little too much, so it's not a bad idea to enlist your higher self to help you overcome some of your bad habits, poor lifestyle or mental and emotional 'handicaps'.

You can again feel intense feelings of affection between the 27th and the 30th. Relationships can be abrupt, passionate, argumentative and also thoroughly fulfilling, all in one day. This is no doubt going to offer you considerable variety but may also frazzle your nerves in the process. Equanimity and a more balanced approach are necessary throughout January.

Romance and friendship

Between the 1st and the 3rd the prescription for success is to disguise your weaknesses. Does this sound a little deceptive? Perhaps. But, as they say, 'all is fair in love and war'. This is the way you'll attract the right sort of people into your life throughout the first few days of 2010.

Recognising the difficulties that arise in a relationship from a lack of compatibility is one thing. However, simply understanding your partner isn't necessarily going to make them any better: they also need to work on themselves. From the 4th to the 8th you need to point this out or accept your relationships for what they are, as quirky as they might be. At the end of the day, as long as you feel happy and confident about them, what's the problem?

Catch a slice of peace between the 10th and the 12th. This is a time to let your hair down, enjoy some easy living, the company of others and, if you can't have that, your own company will be just as sweet.

Sometimes you have to be selfish to grab an opportunity. You might feel as if you're snatching it from someone else. Around the 13th your shrewdness will win out and you'll be satisfied in the process.

Be careful in following someone else's lead around the 15th. A person who wishes to lead you hastily in a certain direction is probably going to end up in a state of chaos. Thankfully you'll be there to help them pick up the pieces.

Even if you're confronted by a contentious dilemma around the 16th to the 18th, you'll be in a perfectly poised state of mind to deal with the problem in a balanced way. In fact, you'll be inviting others to bring their problems to you because you're in that state of mind that easily sees solutions. You'll be appreciated for it.

You might feel frazzled between the 19th and the 23rd because someone is draining your tolerance. You don't necessarily have to be a saint at this time, but your patience will be tested. Even though you are a decent human being as well as forbearing, trying to be nice in the face of someone's insensitivity will most certainly be a challenge for you.

Between the 27th and the 30th, take the initiative in love. Feel balanced in the way you're looking at things, and make yourself immune to being rubbed the wrong way. This can be an exciting close to the first month of the year.

Work and money

You have a high degree of drive and energy and, even if you are only a novice at what you do, you'll be featured for your skills and unusual talents, particularly between the 3rd and the 11th.

Be more effective in demolishing any outdated modes of work, especially after the 16th. The Moon with Neptune on the 18th gives you a creative spin on things and a chance to make yourself and your squad of peers much happier.

It might be a professional anniversary of some sort around the 21st, so celebrate! Invite your friends, co-workers and even family members if you want to commemorate the start of a new path that should now be bringing you the desired fruits of your labour.

You have a wish to copyright or at least protect your ideas after the 29th. This is a time when you don't want any nasty endings to your commercial associations, so protect what is yours and don't be afraid to get others to 'sign on the dotted line' to confirm these facts.

Destiny dates

Positive: 1, 2, 3, 8, 9, 10, 11, 12, 13, 27, 28, 30
Negative: 15, 19, 20, 22, 23
Mixed: 4, 5, 6, 7, 8, 16, 17, 18, 21, 29

Highlights of the month

You could be at odds with others this month and between the 1st and the 9th your mind could feel somewhat confused philosophically and morally. Someone you thought was a friend might hit you with a theological bullet right between the eyes.

There's no use trying to counter this with arguments, debate or even intelligent deduction; they won't listen to you. Some people know it all and there's no way of changing them. It's better to bite your tongue and enjoy the day rather than tying yourself in religious and ethical knots.

Between the 2nd and the 11th you'll be activated by a colleague to use the power of Mars to achieve great success in your work. You could feel there's a hazard with either a business or a political 'animal' who's trying to dictate the terms of your activities. But you won't stand for it, and Venus comes to the rescue after the 17th when it conjoins Jupiter and gives you ample charm to win over these people without having to be confrontational.

Be careful not to let your self-confidence get the better of you, particularly if you're drinking at a social function, because a dramatic leak might cause no end of trouble for you after the 18th.

After the 20th your energy reaches a new high with the Sun returning to your birth chart's natal position. You can expect your physical energy to increase and your confidence to assist you in shining a golden aura that will attract everyone, near and far. This is definitely a period of the year when you can achieve great things.

This month generally will also be an important month for you to reconnect with old friends. A karmic connection can be experienced with someone from your past and if there have been issues that haven't been resolved, it's now time to put aside dead, symbolic logic and connect with them on a heart level.

Romance and friendship

You can attract, sway and even coerce someone you have your eye on from the 2nd till the 5th. They will be an absorbed recipient of your love and attention and will also be happy to reciprocate your gestures of affection.

Be careful after the 8th because the rumours reaching you will not always be coming from the right person. There are other sources of information at this time, so try to find alternatives before making any judgements on things.

You will come out the inevitable master of your circumstances after the 14th. An expected plan can work your way, and it's better to remain silent even if loved ones are prodding and prying you to find out what's on your mind.

Are you leading a contradictory existence? Are you in a state of affairs or circumstances that occur completely against the grain of your thinking or desires? From the 17th you need to end this ambiguous situation once and for all. If this relates to your relationship with a friend or lover and it doesn't completely fulfil you, you know what you have to do.

When the Sun comes to your sign of Pisces around the 19th, you'll have a desire to change who you are. You may even be reflecting on a magazine article or photograph that spurs you on to do something different, to alter your ego and be perceived by others in a completely new light.

Between the 20th and the 24th you will win an argument and come out on top, but this will give you an unfair and probably a punishing advantage over someone. Use this power with integrity.

By the 28th you'll be inspired by a notable spokesperson, someone you hear speak or who happens to cross your path. You will be keen to apply practically some of the insights you gain from this individual.

Work and money

Between the 7th and the 10th, being arrogant in your workplace will undermine your stability, even if you think you've gained the upper hand. If you're torn over a judgement, it's best to let the decision sit for a while and allow your intuition to bring you some answers from within. This will do the trick.

Between the 15th and the 20th you can be a lamp, a shining light for others in sharing information to which you are privy. This will be a time when you feel a greater need for education, to increase the brightness of your inner intellectual light.

From the 19th till the 26th you'll be questioning what you hear and this might not go down too well with others who believe you should simply stomach what they have to say without any recourse to query. Either you or someone else may be obstructed in receiving the truth. Don't allow your ego to dominate the scenario.

Destiny dates

Positive: 11, 14, 15, 16, 28

Negative: 1

Mixed: 2, 3, 4, 5, 6, 7, 8, 9, 10, 17, 18, 19, 20, 21, 22, 23, 24, 25, 26

Highlights of the month

You can tear off your crude masks this month and simply be who you are, even if it is a little wild and whacky. Between the 4th and the 7th, give yourself full permission to enjoy life and discover your inner child. Plenty of surprises are in store for you, with Venus making contact with the forward-thinking and electric Uranus. Your relationships this month will be enthralling, to say the least.

After the 8th, Venus and Mars provide you ample passion with which to enjoy life. Chasing potential lovers, however, will cause you some strain, so the advice of a close friend might help you avoid becoming a jammed wreck.

In the middle of the month, be careful that even a little constructive criticism from you may be classed as sacrilegious, blasphemous, by others. Although you feel justified in saying what you do, your family may have a different view on things. You may not be all that popular around the 16th, so try to keep your views to yourself.

Something you wished to buy this month may seem like a striking sensation but could end up being overpriced. There could be little return for the investments that you make, especially when the Sun moves to your zones of finances around the 21st.

Cryptic messages that you receive trigger some sort of combat by the 22nd in your work sphere. Try not to read too much into what others are saying. You might be creating more trouble than it's worth.

Try to keep your glorious memories alive, even if some of them are not all that pleasurable. You can't smell the rose, as they say, without sometimes suffering the prick of its thorn. On the 24th, take the good with the bad.

The Sun produces excellent results for you professionally as well as in your social sphere after the 29th. Although you may feel as if you have some decreased capital because of your spending habits, a favoured project will give you plenty of opportunity to practise your skills and impress the right people. You may need to initiate some new technology to get the job done, but you'll enjoy the new learning curve and this will award you some respect from your co-workers.

Around the 31st, long revisions may be time consuming. I suggest you don't cut corners with your work, your communications or other interactions, otherwise you'll need to go back and redo everything.

Romance and friendship

You could be hit with a grand plot to improve your love life around the 2nd. From within the depths of your being, an idea may hatch that gives you that brilliant sense of 'ah ha!'. To break through into new territory with your loved one, you may have to endure a few days of hardship, but persistence will pay off and the rewards will be well worth the wait.

From the 6th till the 9th you have wonderful opportunities to mix with others and socialise. Dress to manipulate! It sounds wicked but power is a serious game, especially in the love stakes, and how you look will determine the success or otherwise of your strategy.

Someone may stop being so cosy with you from the 11th. It will be erroneous on your part to try to speed up the process of reconciliation. You have better options available to you after the 14th, especially when the Moon conjoins Jupiter. Bide your time.

You can smell an untruth a mile away, particularly around the 17th when a garbled load of nonsense reflects exactly that—a tall tale. Don't fall prey to the smooth talker. He or she will only break your heart.

If you're incapable of carrying emotional baggage around, why do it any longer? Between the 21st and the 25th, you'll feel ready to drop a bundle of past hurts, guilt and shame. Make a resolution, and let go of it all.

Between the 29th and the 31st you can spread your empire by making as many friends as you can. You may not need to send out a fancy newsletter to announce the changes—the plans you have for becoming bigger, brighter and more popular—but networking will be important and will bring you some profound amusement as well as the popularity you desire.

Work and money

Even a moderate amount of sexuality will not be tolerated between the 2nd and the 6th—workplace sexuality, that is. Integrity is probably not written into the constitution of your workplace, but it will be something you'll need to enforce and remind someone of at this time, especially if it happens to be a boss or someone in a superior position to you.

Deals are looming on the horizon between the 7th and the 9th. Don't scatter yourself running around in circles but focus on the one idea that will bring you the best financial remuneration.

Work at this time will require a constant assessment of your abilities and the prevailing trends, particularly between the 15th and the 19th.

After the 21st an upswing in your finances will be a welcome relief, but by the same token, a strange incident in your workplace may also occur that will require you to keep your cool. You should remain tight-lipped about extracurricular activities, especially if you're on the prowl for a new job or better income. Trust no one at this time.

Around the 25th, enemies may cause problems. Those whom you thought were there to support you will abandon their cover and reveal their true intentions.

Destiny dates

Positive: 8, 9, 14, 23, 24, 29, 30

Negative: 3, 11, 25

Mixed: 2, 4, 5, 6, 7, 15, 16, 17, 18, 19, 21, 22, 25, 31

Highlights of the month

An act of spontaneous mercy is the mark of someone who truly has developed, and expresses, compassion. Between the 1st and the 7th you will have the opportunity to transform yourself further through your assistance to someone else. Mind you, a newcomer on the scene may be somewhat of a wildcard, one might say a cuckoo, but your compassion and sensitivity will extend to helping even those who are a little bit 'left of the dial'.

You can resurrect friendships after the 8th and this will bring a smile to your face. Be careful not to follow distorted guidelines that don't necessarily apply to your personal scenario. Trust your own intuition when it comes to making judgements about friends this month. Cutting corners, leapfrogging tasks, will be a shallow approach to achieving your professional and financial objectives. You may have to work long hours by the 20th and communications could be tedious, but you'll be on top of it and get the upper hand.

Around the 23rd, a question may arise: how will you get out of an unauthorised slip up? You may have done something on the sly, thinking no one will notice, which could result in a bit of a dumb breakdown on your part. It's you, your thinking and attitudes that will continue to contribute to any saga that is bothering you.

Having a vague belief isn't going to cut it anymore. You're either in or out on the 25th. This applies as much to relationships as it does to philosophy, peer groups and to any other circumstance in which you are walking the fence. Fortunately, by the 26th you've developed enough insight to make a clear decision and this will afford you a sigh of relief.

Children with scattered energies are a problem between the 27th and the 30th. If they've become bogged down in a stuffy routine you'll need to work on new ways to revitalise their creativity as well as your own in the process.

Towards the end of the month you may need to prune your newly hatched plan because some of the details are a little bit 'woolly around the edges'. Listen to the feedback you get from others, even if they are younger, because they may have some brilliant insights into how to polish an otherwise rough diamond.

Romance and friendship

Between the 2nd and the 5th someone may approach you to try to point out the error of your perception in some sort of friendship or personal arrangement with which you are continuing. You may have been isolating yourself through a continuing belief in an illusion. You must rid yourself of this.

Around the 8th it could be that time of the year when someone does an annual dump of their emotional stuff on you. You know what I'm talking about, Pisces! Your Sun sign is the one that tends to say 'yes' to all and sundry, when they have no one else to turn to with their own problems. Protect yourself, especially by the 10th, when the Moon and Neptune cause you to absorb negative energies.

Short, written statements will be more effective in driving your point home around the 15th, especially if you don't want to deal with others in a one-on-one, face to face situation. Your ability to see the good in people between the 17th and 21st is a noteworthy practice and one that others should diligently inquire into if they too would hope to become better friends and universal lovers like Pisceans. You will help transform someone throughout this important cycle.

You could be more thorough in your requests on the 22nd and, if this relates to family members not pulling their weight on the home front, you can deliver the optimum effect by speaking your mind.

If you need to participate in some sort of pow-wow as a mediator after the 26th, you must do so as a pragmatic participant. Don't let your airy-fairy beliefs or philosophical views impact on the discussion. This is most important if you are dealing with children who haven't yet had the experience that you have.

A rash explanation on the 28th will dash your hopes at reconciliation or of finding a resolution. Take your time and don't be afraid to repeat yourself two, three or even four times to make sure others understand your point of view.

Work and money

There's nothing worse than a scattered launch of a new product, enterprise or concept. This could be the case between the 6th and the 10th, so be careful in collecting your ideas, cohesively stringing the concepts together and supplying a simple process for others to adhere to. You may be misreading them if you think they're going to be able to take the initiative all on their own.

Between the 16th and the 20th, someone is frivolous but nevertheless fun on the work front. You'll feel as if you can afford to enjoy a few quiet chuckles with a co-worker and still meet your deadlines. A mystery may be pulsing somewhere within your workplace and you won't be able to put your finger on it. This could bother you between the 24th and the 26th, but try to skip to your own business rather than try to work out where everyone else is or what they're doing.

You want to express your principles and ethics between the 28th and the 30th, mainly because your boss might try to shoot down the welfare of you and your colleagues. Unless you speak up, that may happen. Courage will be the name of the game in the last few days of April.

Destiny dates

Positive: 1, 16, 17, 18, 19, 21, 22

Negative: 9, 10, 27

Mixed: 2, 3, 4, 5, 6, 7, 8, 15, 20, 23, 24, 25, 26, 28, 29, 30

Highlights of the month

After the 2nd you mustn't get too wound up or emotional about your appointments and meetings this month. You are committed to your work and will do almost anything to gain top marks for the services you perform. With Jupiter and Uranus combining in your Sun sign, you want to do things bigger and better than everyone else.

By the 9th you may feel as if you're living a trapped existence. But this is all in your mind. It's quite likely your domestic or social situation is suffocating you, namely because you don't have enough space in which to be yourself. This may not be easily remedied due to financial constraints, so you need to connect with your nearest and dearest, your lover or spouse, and allow your mental and emotional space to act as a substitute for the physical space you may not be able to have as soon as you would like.

There's a wasteful controller who dominates your

professional climate around the 12th, which could cause you some frustration, particularly with Saturn having re-entered your zone of relationships. You could make a transparent discovery, but an obvious substitution may have to be avoided because those who pull the strings will disagree with you.

On the 19th you'll realise that an enemy has limited power, so you mustn't feed too much fuel to that fire of concern. Be careful that your well-intentioned, pure searches for truth and purpose don't end up becoming meaningless. Seek answers in the practical book of experience to gain relevant solutions.

Speaking of books, textbook fashion won't reflect who you are, either. As Venus triangulates your Sun sign, it's a great omen to portray yourself in the most beautiful way possible by the 25th. You don't need to follow fads blindly to attract others. Try to recollect that axiom that says 'beauty is skin deep' before venturing forth to the local mall and spending huge amounts of money trying to make yourself into something you just aren't.

Between the 29th and the 31st some of the planetary positions cause you to doubt yourself. Saturn will go direct, indicating you will have to digest fully some of the responsibilities you've been avoiding for a while. At the same time, Neptune, the planet of ideals and spirituality, moves into its reverse motion. When dealing with others, try to get to the bottom line. They may dance you around, spin you a yarn and play mind games. Dusty guarantees are the last thing you need now.

Romance and friendship

You are quite emotional this month and particularly between the 1st and the 3rd you may make an unsafe resolution. Rather than announcing what you're going to do to others, might I suggest that you keep the resolve to yourself so that you don't get egg on your face?

If you want to impress people between the 8th and the 12th, you should try being a little bit more abstract in your tactics. Don't reveal your hand too quickly. This will create an air of mystery around what you say, what you do and how you appear. You're sure to snare someone into your web of love or lust, particularly if you are a single Piscean.

After the 17th you mustn't let your flagging nerves stop you from participating in some event, as eccentric or way out as it may seem. You could be an independent novice in the arena to which you are invited, but this will be a lot of fun and it will eventually open your eyes, mind and heart to a whole lot of new opportunities in your life.

Between the 20th and the 21st some relief will arrive at last! If you've been shouldering some responsibilities by yourself, and finding very little support, especially at home. This can now turn a corner.

What's your antidote to an offender around the 23rd? When someone constantly berates you, takes subtle swipes at your character, and so on, it becomes difficult to know whether or not to coat yourself in armour and let things slide off it, or smash them over the head with a sledgehammer! It's probably best to be quietly assertive and not react too strongly. You need to show that you are not fazed by childish remarks.

Between the 30th and the 31st, constrain your pride. You will feel as if you need to 'up the ante' to make you feel equal to others. But this can work against you, with others seeing you as a braggart or, worse still, insecure about yourself in their company.

Work and money

Unpopular targets could leave you and your work colleagues reeling, but sometimes what is good is not necessarily pleasant. Try to look at the upside of things from the 5th to the 9th.

Reforming others will strike a chord with you around the 19th, but unless you have powerful allies who are in concert with you, your activities will seem obsolete, to say the least. You will need to reform yourself first and remember, as they say, 'charity begins at home'.

Joint finances take a front seat from the 23rd till the 27th. Not only will you have to contend with your partner about how and why you are spending what you spend, but you could feel like mud the morning after if you don't curb your expenses.

In the competitive stakes, especially around the 30th, the one with the highest volume will win.

Speak up and speak up louder so that you can be heard above everyone else. Once you get enough attention, you can close the deal to your satisfaction.

Destiny dates

Positive: 11, 20, 21

Negative: 19, 24, 26, 27, 29

Mixed: 1, 2, 3, 5, 6, 7, 8, 9, 10, 12, 17, 23, 25, 30, 31

Highlights of the month

The start of the month is not particularly good for your attitude towards relationships. Saturn, Mars and also Neptune could have you wondering whether or not marriage and committed love is perhaps simply a dreary invention thrust upon us as a test. These feelings will most certainly pass but up till the 5th you'll need to find a more constructive way to deal with these thoughts.

Startling honesty will come to the fore after the 8th when Jupiter enters your zone of speech and finances. Speaking truthfully about how you feel rather than burying your feelings under a mountain of frustration will be the best policy. With Saturn continuing to pass through your zone of partnerships, many lessons are going to be learned. This is a time when service, sacrifice and 'wearing the other person's shoes' for a time are essential for the improvement of your friendships and more intimate relationships.

Venus passes into your zone of work and daily routine after the 14th. Don't let the damaging arrows of competition or envy impact upon your workplace relationships. Yes, there may be some discouraging problems you need to confront; but once again, transparency will bring some good results, especially after the 16th. You can collaborate and, with well-directed ideas, you can cement your friendships positively once again.

You are super-creative by the 19th but don't let these impulses exhaust you. You need to know which ideas to latch onto and which ones to let fall by the wayside. You can't waste your valuable time and resources on every single notion that comes to mind. Nor can you afford to waste valuable energy in the same way, on people who are not going to be around forever. You need to prioritise during the month of June.

If the Earth seems to have become a grey, stale planet, you have a responsibility to shine your light and uplift others, which you can do after the 21st. You'll be feeling innovative and will want to employ these creative aspects of your personality in all of your endeavours and in your personal relationships. Also after the 21st, when Venus creates excellent aspects to your professional sphere, you have an opportunity to look at the alternatives by way of employment. This could be a fundamental transition in your life and one that should be fully embraced.

On the 26th, a lunar eclipse occurs in your zone

of friendships and also profitability. This means you can't preserve the current state of affairs without some feeling of lacklustre. Change is essential, so a dynamic push forward should be wholeheartedly initiated with a view to improving your general life-style.

Romance and friendship

On the 4th someone could divert your attention in a completely different direction. This could be just what you need to lift up your spirits and help you forget about your concerns, even the negligible ones.

You'll want to extend yourself around the 6th by doing something for someone, a favour, such as looking after their three kids. You'll be so glad after you've dealt with them that they aren't your own! Harmony truly is accessible if you want it, but if you keep taking on the woes of the world, what exactly don't you understand about finding yourself run ragged by doing all of these sorts of favours for everyone?

Between the 7th and the 9th you can make breakthroughs in your relationships by getting closer to the ones you love. However, repeatedly studying an axiom—a truth or some special phrase, like a mantra—is the only way you can live what you learn. There has to be a practical application of the do-it-yourself, self-help books available in the marketplace. Simply studying words will not work. Apply what you learn, even if it feels a little uncom-fortable at first.

You have a chance to take a privileged dig at someone and, even though you don't mean anything by it, your sense of humour could go straight over their heads around the 11th. Pick your mark before opening your mouth.

Between the 13th and the 17th you'll need to demonstrate that your words are productive in your friendships. If you're simply 'talking the talk' and not 'walking the walk', you're going to lose credibility. But you are the sort of person who lives by what they preach, so this shouldn't be too much of a problem and will in fact endear others to you.

The Sun conjoins your romance zone on the 21st, so for many Piscean-born individuals, this could be the threshold of a startling new relationship or at least a shift in attitude. You need to put out feelers to find people who are resonating on your same level or vibration.

After the 27th, even if you're a bloke, you may want to renew your cooking skills so that you can share your love and creativity in the kitchen with a few close friends. This is a special social occasion in which food may play an important role.

Work and money

Materialise your thoughts and plans by working more carefully with your diary between the 4th and the 6th. You can't afford to forget meetings, arrangements and appointment dates and times. You will show your professionalism by paying careful attention to this aspect of your life.

Numerous diagnoses will be necessary to ferret out any wrong areas of your monetary management between the 8th and the 14th. These may not be serious blunders but down the track they can become tediously time consuming. It's best to sort out the small stuff now so that the situation doesn't snowball into anything more serious.

Just remember, once an icon doesn't mean an icon forever. You should work for the sake of work itself and not for any fame or glory. These issues will be paramount in your mind between the 15th and the 19th. Doing good work will give you satisfaction.

If you feel like you're working for a clumsy corporation, then you must do something about it between the 24th and the 28th. Don't just moan about your dissatisfaction; get in there and apply yourself towards improving things.

Destiny dates

Positive: 4, 15, 16, 17, 18, 19, 21

Negative: Nil

Mixed: 5, 6, 7, 8, 9, 10, 11, 12, 13, 14, 24, 25, 26, 27, 28

Highlights of the month

Do you feel as if you have enough knowledge just now, Pisces? You'll need as much wisdom as you can muster to deal with the enlivening energies of Saturn and Mars combining in your relationship sphere.

You will continue to experience problems as long as you resist the major transition I've been speaking about for you this year. Embrace any sort of unstable twist of affairs that happens to arise. The series of events that occur in your relationship this month will actually be blessings in disguise.

After the 9th you'll need to observe and analyse carefully the state of your relationships. A gradual evaluation of things is superior to hasty, knee jerk reactions in which we are likely to falter and misjudge the characters, but more importantly the intentions, of those who count. Unless you are able to synthesise your observations carefully, you might find yourself in a bit of a dip by the 18th. You'll need a multiple push, a two- or three-pronged attack, to deal with these issues.

Actually, in some cases, it may not be you who is having the problem. With these planetary energies affecting your partner or spouse, there may be considerable frustration or disappointment in their lives and you will have to deal with this. You'll be called upon to offer advice, to support that person emotionally and fortunately you are born under the perfectly compassionate sign of Pisces and will be better equipped than most people to do your best through this stage of their life.

The focus shifts from your personal relation-ships to your financial commitments after the 21st. You could probably welcome a distorted percep-tion about the way things are, but that would only continue to keep you attached to the 'slave maze' to which many are now addicted. What do I mean by this? Well, most people find it easy just to follow the crowd, to confuse themselves with jargon, vain hopes and promises, without really investigating things for themselves.

In the matter of money, especially your joint finances, you mustn't thrust aside any warnings your intuition feeds you. Listen carefully to that inner voice because it will have some vital informa-tion that can help you in your commercial activities, investments and means of earning. Moreover, you'll be more agreeable with your partner over how money should be saved and spent.

Romance and friendship

You don't have to deal with an impossible philosopher on the 1st; just listen to them and nod your head. You don't have to agree with anything and you don't have to feel railroaded into shifting your position on a belief system. As long as you're respectful and perhaps even pretend a little bit, you'll even enjoy the banter you get into with someone around this time.

You may be wondering about the dilemma of a friend, the circumstances surrounding someone in your peer group and will finally get the official word around the 4th to the 6th. Even if what you hear is not so palatable to you, at least the circumstances will be resolved and you and everyone else can move on.

You'll find yourself in the middle of a classic crowd of people sometime between the 14th and the 19th. You'll be called upon to act in an expert, social manner and therefore brushing up on your etiquette will be necessary. The people with whom you will be engaged may even be the upper crust or crème de la crème of society.

You'll need some initial proof before giving your heart to someone around the 23rd. Love could be calling on you, but don't make the same mistakes as before. There's no harm in putting someone to the test, to test their mettle.

You could be ferreting out information from the past from the 26th till the 28th. Interestingly, an unconnected story will shed some light on your own current life themes and issues. This could be a TV show, an off-the-cuff discussion, or a book you're reading. In any case, the wisdom you gain from it will be very elevating and revealing of your own life history.

Around the 29th, give yourself full permission to enjoy a mental vacuum that will be very attractive and appealing, indeed. There's nothing like your own space, especially when that space is completely uncluttered. Enjoy it, you deserve it.

Around the 31st you'll need a radical shoulder to lean on or perhaps even to cry on. Your issues may not be the normal run-of-the-mill story the average person can understand or help you with. But the universe will provide you with someone who can help you at this time and who has a lateral approach to life and problem solving.

Work and money

You need to descend into the deepest recesses of your creative self between the 1st and the 4th and by doing so will be able to come up with some scintillating, brilliant ideas to present to your work-mates and professional advisors. You'll be ready and raring to go, full of beans and vitality, and able to complete your tasks as required.

You must hear the framework of a concept before understanding the nuts and bolts of a proposal offered to you between the 6th and the 10th. If this requires you to put quite a bit on the line, listen more carefully and don't be rushed into a decision.

You know, sometimes people want to skip the pain but in the process they also miss out on the sweetness. Around the 16th you may be tempted to cut corners, to sidestep an issue that is probably a little too hard to bear. Don't do that. Be prepared to take on the challenge and in so doing you'll experience some wonderful, unexpected circumstances and people as a part of this process.

You may have little patience for dealing with those who wish to tear you down after the 21st. Around the 24th your words may be like paprika, biting and cutting right to the heart of the problem or the person concerned.

If you're a person in a position of power, your seniority won't stop you from having some fun between the 29th and the 31st. A social event involving work could bring lots of smiles to your face.

Destiny dates

Positive: 2, 3, 4, 5, 6, 7, 8, 9, 10, 14, 15, 17, 19, 26, 27, 28, 29, 30

Negative: Nil

Mixed: 1, 16, 18, 21, 23, 24, 31

AUGUST

Highlights of the month

The saying used to be: 'The British are coming! The British are coming!' But this month you'll be crying: 'Venus and Mercury are coming! Venus and Mercury are coming!' And thank goodness, too, because these two wonderful planets will bring a dose of sweetness to your love life, to your friendships, and to your family interactions as well.

If there is any competition, you'll be doing it recreationally. By the 9th it's not a bad idea to use humour to overcome any feelings of inadequacy or coolness in your love life. You may even want to splurge a little by the 10th and show a token of your appreciation by buying gifts for the ones you love most.

Try not to make too much of an empty incident around the 16th or 17th. Things happen in life and, when you look at them in an unbiased fashion, you realise that usually the troubles you have are to a large extent superimposed by your own thinking and concepts. This is exactly what may happen. So learn from the past; don't be an unaware historian. By studying the past you'll be able to overcome the drawbacks you've experienced and move forward without carrying a heap of baggage around with you based upon fear and rejection.

Someone has commercially infringed upon you, taken advantage of you, or out and out lied or stolen from you. They may be caught out and this can work to your advantage after the 20th. Don't let them patronise you; you know the truth and should speak out. Let them know exactly where you stand and specifically the hot water they are in. This is a time of victory for you over your competitors and those who would otherwise try to harm you.

The collective work station could get a little crowded at your job around the 26th. Maybe you should make yourself a little scarce, get some quality 'me' time and leave the work crowd to its own devices rather than getting embroiled in an arising crossfire. I suggest you give them the slip. The Sun is powerful for you by the 30th and at this time you may even be asked to sit in officially for someone of a higher rank at a function or meeting. You'll do well, so don't allow your self-doubt to interfere with a positive outcome.

Romance and friendship

There's safety and power in numbers and between the 2nd and the 7th your idea to rally friends and relatives to a cause is a good one. 'Many hands make light work' and so by enlisting the help of a group, you can drastically reduce the time you spend dealing with trifling matters. Of course, the goal is to make much more time for pleasure and passion!

By the 9th you may feel as if you're living a trapped existence. But this is all in your mind. It's quite likely your domestic or social situation is suffocating you, perhaps because you don't have enough space in which to be yourself.

Your lame protests are not going to change anything, however. You know that. You have very little control over the way others do things, so it's best to remain unassuming and non-committal if someone asks your opinion about something that you know will only stir up trouble.

A taboo will be appealing around the 13th when a compatible vice brings you and another person together. This may be as harmless as eating ice cream and chocolate, but it will still be fun and give you the feeling you're stepping outside the square and extending yourself into a no-go area without actually doing any harm. Enjoy the opportunity.

A friend may be prone to nitpicking and this will get on your nerves around the 20th. If it's 'that time of the month', so to speak, you may explode in a reactive retort, but it's best to bite your tongue and let it blow over.

For the singles among you, adventure will verse chastity after the 22nd. A sense of discovery will pervade your mind and your friendships so it's quite likely you'll naturally be drawn to interesting people, those from a different culture, possibly even travellers who are crossing your path.

On the 25th it may be hard to restrict and discipline yourself if you're working towards a coveted trophy. This sounds like work, doesn't it? In fact, we're still in the right section of your August forecast, and this August trophy may simply relate to health, a state of mind, or inner spiritual wellbeing. Once again, restricting and disciplining yourself is the only way you can achieve an improved state of affairs in any area of life.

You need to commit yourself and others in your family to a regular round of debate to clear the air on the domestic scene. Around the 30th it will be a good idea to lay your cards on the table and ask others to do the same. Contrary to what you feel, there won't be an argument and this will in fact invite people to share openly some of those feelings they thought would not be accepted. This will serve to increase love, harmony and understanding between all of you.

Work and money

Between the 5th and the 9th a slippery request on the work front could leave you writhing, uncomfortable and unsure just how to respond. Put the problem on the tin roof for the moment and wait for the right circumstances in which to give your answer. Better still, you should employ one of the laws of power, which is to get others to do the dirty work for you.

If someone switches to a lie around the 13th, you can rest assured this is a sign of their invisible pride. You may catch them out on something that is perhaps not very significant but which definitely reveals a different side to their character.

By the 24th you'll be fortunate enough to access some important resource that will help you sidestep an unexpected overnight pile of work. This in turn makes you eligible for a vacation—well, at least a few days off, anyhow—especially around the 30th.

Destiny dates

Positive: 2, 3, 4, 13, 24, 25, 30
Negative: 16, 17, 26
Mixed: 5, 6, 7, 9, 20, 22, 13

Highlights of the month

There's no problem going it alone this month. Mercury and the Sun give you the power to convince others of your position. Mercury is retrograde, which still warns that you should be careful not to sign on the dotted line if you're not completely clear on the terms and conditions of some agreement. But an unreadable prediction doesn't necessarily mean you're not correct about your assumptions. You could be challenged by someone who seems to think they know more than you do, but you should trust your experience and innate wisdom as being correct.

Your acute translation of circumstances is probably too close to the bone when it comes to advising a friend this month. Between the 3rd and the 9th you'll be called upon to mediate, advise or possibly even chastise those who've been ill-behaved and those who do not understand the cause of their problems. It may be unbearable deciding on a course of action or perhaps how you will treat your friend in future. But sometimes you have to 'be cruel to be kind'.

On the topic of friends, your past may still be bobbing up and down in your mind. An old friend may be more forgiving nowadays so I suggest you give them a little more latitude if they have somehow been trying to make their way back into your life. Allow the quality of your forgiveness to give them a second chance. Friendship and promoting or fostering goodwill between yourself and others is spotlighted around the 19th.

Your principal goal this month should be to express your individuality without upsetting the status quo. Venus, Mars, Saturn, Uranus and Jupiter all interact to produce some rather tense moments for you, but imaginary disadvantages are exactly that! Don't think negatively about your position in the larger scheme of things. Hold your head up; approach your superiors with an air of authority. They will respect you for it.

The second half of the month is most interesting in that you meet new people who are just so different to your usual group. This will fascinate you and draw you into a deeper and more long-lasting friendship with at least one of them.

Believe me, the strangest of romantic alliances sometimes work, so don't be too quick to judge a stranger you meet who probably seems like chalk and cheese when it comes to comparing your personalities.

Romance and friendship

Observing others is an idiotic study only if the people you happen to be observing are idiots. And this is how you may feel between the 5th and the 9th, when you find yourself among people who are completely outside of your normal cultural framework. But you can still offer some sort of pleasing creation by way of words or demeanour that can inspire others.

You need to work on your inner pool of creativity and show it to the world. You can act as a mentor, a guide or, interestingly enough, a benchmark for someone junior to you between the 11th and the 15th. A friendship may develop out of your mutual respect, even though there is a rather large gap in age between you.

Worries and trifles are only bothering you around the 16th because of the approach of the Moon to Pluto. What this means is that you are focusing too much on the minutiae rather than the bigger picture of a situation.

This year it could appear as if the universe has placed a large magnifying glass in front of your eyes to see the obvious flaws in people around you. Remember to accept people warts and all because this is part of the process of love. Wouldn't you want them to do likewise if they had the same giant lens looking at you?

Cultivate flexibility in your relationships between the 19th and the 21st when your ideals could be at loggerheads with the reality of the situation. If you keep trying to force someone to be like you, it's never going to work. Rather, bend, stretch and accommodate the idiosyncrasies of your friends and lovers.

The Moon will conjoin Jupiter and Uranus on the 23rd and this, being in your Sun sign, is a wonderful omen for bringing out a little bit of wackiness or good humour and harmless madness. You'll be attractive and others will want to be part of the game of life that you are playing at this time. 'Eat, drink and be merry' seems to be the prevailing theme for you right now, but be careful not to take it to extremes.

Work and money

You'd hate to become economically scarred if you opted for the pawn shop during a moment of financial distress, wouldn't you? Hold onto your valuables, particularly after the 5th, even if you feel as though the bills are mounting and you need to off-load some items of sentimental value.

The tide will turn, particularly when the planet Venus enters your zone of great fortune around the 9th. This could be a time when your worries could be relaxed in this respect.

The 11th could be a rather wiry day so you need to practise some meditation, deep breathing or other relaxation exercises to help decompress a situation at work.

For some, simply saying they're not going to be a spendthrift is not going to work. It's probably better to devise a careful management strategy of your spending habits, especially around the 18th. This way you'll have the best of both worlds. You'll be able to spend but, by controlling that spending, you won't be too out of pocket at the end of the month when the credit card bill arrives.

Between the 21st and the 24th you must understand that an isolated protest won't stand up by itself and you will need some allies behind you. Before trying to fight city hall you need to make sure others feel the same way as you do. At least this way you have a chance of presenting a convincing argument to your superiors. There is strength in numbers.

Destiny dates

Positive: 12, 13, 14, 15

Negative: 16, 20

Mixed: 3, 4, 5, 6, 7, 8, 9, 11, 18, 19, 21, 22, 23, 24

Highlights of the month

Please don't be scared of your bills this month. The Sun and Saturn create a greater sense of responsibility over your finances, but you must see those bills as a reflection of the great privileges you have in life. Just think of it: electricity, shelter, food, transport, outings, travels, fashion and other enjoyments are all made possible by the fact that you have bills to show just how much you've been honoured in terms of your experiences, comfort and enjoyments.

Try not to let your suspicions get the better of you by the 5th. These may be unfounded and could cause a friend or family member to retaliate. You may need to make a discrete exit to avoid a dispute.

On another front, probably socially or even professionally, a slippery gesture could catch you off guard. You should beware the flatterer because he or she feeds you with an empty spoon.

By the 19th you have a grand opportunity to overcome some of your phobias. Even ingrained habits can be dealt with and eliminated once and for all. Meditation, or better still, hypnosis can be the solution by going deeply into your subconscious, discovering the causes of your fears and then eliminating them, one by one, freeing you of the past.

Around the 23rd, when the Sun enters the ninth house, try to think carefully about educational pursuits that you feel compelled to pursue. You may have very little time to allocate to any new commitment like this and, most importantly, remember that a 'dead graduate' is of no use to anyone. In other words, driving yourself into the ground simply to inflate your ego with a handful of merit certificates is not the most practical solution.

Your constructive vision is growing and in particular after the 24th you will feel the full weight of your responsibilities on your shoulders, but you need to remind yourself that, 'what doesn't kill you makes you stronger'. In other words, all eyes will be upon you at this critical point in the year, when you will be called upon to show mastery of your talents, to lead others both professionally and ethically, and to balance all this with the other personal requirements that you have in life, namely your family and friends.

A mixture of effects is likely by the 28th when Mars, the power planet, enters your professional zone. You must pick your queries carefully and under no circumstances should you act upon misguided arrangements. Check and double-check the source of information that is offered to you right now. If you ask a question in a state of folly, your credibility could be impacted upon. You mustn't jeopardise your professional integrity at all.

When the Sun conjoins Venus on the 29th, spiritual issues will be tantamount in your mind. A downhill spiritual spiral is the last thing you want. Paying special attention to your inner needs is not a bad idea at this time, especially if you feel as though you've been spreading yourself thinly.

Romance and friendship

Passions are somewhat squashed this month, at least for the first two or three days during the joining of the Sun and Saturn in your sexual zone. After the 4th, however, the Venus and Mars conjunction powers up your lustful energies and it would appear that the ultimate destination during this cycle would be your bedroom!

On the 7th a scarlet mistake will have others embarrassed for you. Choose your words carefully, especially if you're in the company of those whose reactions you're not too familiar with.

You need to dust off your memories between the 11th and the 15th because you have a tendency to allow history to repeat itself. You may have forgotten the pain of a particular relationship only to be reminded when it's too late of just how inept or possibly even insensitive someone from your past really was. Go through the annals of your past connections before accepting a date at this time.

It looks like you'll be co-ordinating a million-and-one things between the 18th and the 20th. You'll want to take the initiative and be seen to be proactive with your family or social group but may actually 'bite off more than you can chew'. If you're involved in clubs or other affiliations this will be an extremely busy time during which the Sun and Saturn conjunction adds responsibilities to your rather full plate as well.

Don't abandon your dreams, even if they're slow in coming to fruition. Around the 23rd you'll have a sneak preview of what's possible, which will deter you from ditching your vision just because it hasn't materialised as quickly as you thought it would. Someone you least expect will now be a part of your future.

You have plenty of sunshine to pedal among friends and strangers alike from the 28th till the 30th. This time you'll be in a perfect position to travel to places where you will make instant connections and realise just how much you've been missing out on.

You will also find yourself learning about the skills you didn't realise you had, socially speaking.

Work and money

How could you possibly work in peace if you don't stop being paranoid about officials and people you think are looking over your shoulder and breathing down your neck? This could be the case on the 3rd, the 7th and also the 11th when you become way too emotional for your own good. You mustn't project your own feelings of inadequacy onto others who are simply doing their job and probably don't understand why you are acting so strangely.

A private tutor is not a bad thing to consider around the 10th, particularly if you're feeling as if you're lagging behind in some area of knowledge. Remember, you can also opt for an online or home-tutoring service, which will work in beautifully with your lifestyle and busy schedule.

Dealing with a philosophical or professional fascist is not going to be much fun between the 18th and the 20th, especially if it's someone who's been called in to make radical changes in the workplace. Stay out of their way and don't even bother trying to change their minds. That will be an exercise in futility.

A better state of affairs can be expected around the 29th and 30th when you do have an expert encounter with someone who at last understands what they're talking about and doesn't have too big an ego, which is a refreshing change.

Destiny dates

Positive: 10, 23, 29, 30
Negative: 1, 2, 3, 5, 6, 7, 11, 12, 13, 14, 15, 24
Mixed: 4, 18, 19, 20, 28

Highlights of the month

Fuzzy marketing, unclear communication and other confusing signals may create a vast gulf between you and someone else with whom you want to be close. Even if you now try to force something to happen with them, when in the past you ignored your own insights and the lessons surrounding them, how can you possibly make it work now or revive it, if it's already dead? Look at things fairly and squarely throughout the month of November, especially after the 8th when Venus the planet of love enters the transformational zone of your horoscope.

Sexual energies, power, joint finances and other shared resources will be extremely important and need to be discussed and worked on. Don't let someone who sarcastically rubs you up the wrong way draw you into expressing the worst side of your personality.

After the 16th, a convenient cure is not necessarily the best course of action for the ailment that plagues you. Why not try some other alternative remedies? However, under all circumstances double-check what you are planning to do with your practitioner, particularly if you are taking other medications, too.

An unexpected sitting, a meeting that has been unscheduled, could catch you off guard around the 22nd. You need to be prepared well in advance and have your facts and figures to hand in a moment's notice. Try not to express your emotions verbally, even if you feel like it. A calm, cool demeanour will win the day. Quiet, calculative assertion will help you master others and be a smashing success.

Travel is on the cards for you this month. If inappropriate lunch breaks haven't added up to enough of what you'd consider reasonable time out, you need to split and 'head for the hills'. If you have a committed partner, they may also be feeling the same and this is a great time to scat! Spend some time on a beach doing nothing or, better still, have a few cosy, candlelit romantic dinners to while away the time.

If you do choose to venture away, when you return it's important for you to ask yourself whether you've been working hard or working smart? My feeling is that it's better to 'sweat cleverly'. This offers you the best of both worlds.

Romance and friendship

You can be a popular hit with your friends on the 1st, the 3rd and the 5th, but only if you step outside your weekday reality and don't go it alone. If your ordinary life feels a little stale, these few days in the beginning of November will set a new pace, ramp up the energy levels and give you an exhilarating sense that there are alternatives to life. Unless you 'seize the day', you're not going to experience anything different.

You have a chance to bury a situation for good after the 8th. This is an excellent thing to do but you must do it on every level of your being. You can't leave any loose threads lying around to tug on you in the future. This is a period also where someone—a friend or even a sibling—may act as a catalyst in helping you overcome an episode that has been draining you for sometime. This will make you feel twenty years younger!

From the 14th till the 19th, humour will be a wonderful weapon that is at your disposal any time you choose. You'll find yourself in an amusing ploy, perhaps working in concert with a couple of friends, playing some practical jokes, entertaining each other or possibly even going out to enjoy some humour or live theatre.

Acknowledge a courtesy that is given to you between the 22nd and the 26th because this will reciprocate goodwill to the person who has done you a good turn.

Dealing with unwanted mail will also include the advances of someone you're not particularly inter-ested in around the 30th. You need to use some diplomacy to get them off your trail.

Work and money

Sometimes you have to be selfish to grab an opportunity, especially if you feel as if you're snatching it from someone else. Around the 3rd you may well get someone's back up by doing just that. If this is a romantic competition, shrewdness will win out.

You'll be satisfied with your finances by around the 7th but you do need to prioritise your schedule, particularly if there are some indecipherable lines in contracts and other pieces of correspondence that have landed on your desk.

It'll be 'head down and rear end up' for you from the 10th to the 12th. A nice but troublesome individual may be very distracting around the 14th. This sort of unwanted attention will continue and probably get on your nerves for a while, not because the person is doing any harm but just because they happen to be an annoying individual.

Power, authority and the pre-acquisition of a new position is likely after the 22nd; however, some sort of accidental infringement could put a damper on the situation. Pay all of your parking and speeding fines and get your filing system in order.

Destiny dates

Positive: 1, 3, 5, 7, 8, 10, 11, 12, 15, 17, 18, 19, 23, 24, 25, 26

Negative: 30

Mixed: 14, 16, 22

Highlights of the month

December is a great month for you—an excellent vibration will suffuse your being and allow you to complete 2010 with a feeling of great success and self-esteem. But it may be measured. Of course, with the Sun transiting the upper part of your horoscope, it's hardly likely you'll have much time for anything else other than work, at least up until the 8th when friends rally around and also urge you to stop becoming floppy around the edges. You may sign up for a new exercise regime and decide to merge your gym membership with a little bit of social time as well.

With Christmas around the corner, there could be something desirable about personal limits. I mean, too much partying, too much eating and drinking, does require a bit of careful discipline and that would have its upside, wouldn't it? 'Like what?', you ask. Isn't it obvious? It will be less weight, a trim, taut figure, and a greater feeling of control over your mind and senses.

When the Sun squares Jupiter around the 17th, just before Christmas you might decide to dump those temporary resolutions to keep fit and to pull back. Why not? The Sun and Jupiter indicate a certain amount of waste, spend-thriftiness, over eating and way too much drinking. Enjoy the few days up until the 30th when the planets Mars and Saturn caution you to be a little bit more careful again.

Overall, however, you will have received an invaluable boost to your knowledge base and your insight and understanding of people as well as yourself this year. Incidentally, your charm will work wonders for you, with your boss overlooking some of your weak points at this late stage of the year.

Finally, my last recommendation for you is that a lost collaboration shouldn't be grieved over for too long. You'll come to see that offloading what you have done, the dead wood in your life, will make your journey much lighter into the new year, into an even better and more fulfilling 2011.

Romance and friendship

A momentary decline in your sense of power, persuasiveness and popularity is nothing to be worried about. This is temporary and by the 3rd your disposition should be back on track with some wonderful opportunities to connect with the right sort of people by around the 7th or 8th.

You will be attractive and will appeal to others between the 10th and 13th. You might be tempted to take some short cuts, to cut corners and possibly even abuse the trust given to you if you have the opportunity. Don't make the mistake of playing with fire. With additional power comes an even greater responsibility, remember that.

You'll have an unrivalled disposition among your peers as the Moon conjoins Jupiter on the 14th, with a touch of the bizarre elevating you to new heights of optimism around the same time. This is due to the lunar and Uranus combination and Mars and Pluto also coming together in your zone of friendships.

However, be careful with this rather intense planetary union because it can cause some battles of wills and also arguments leading up to the 19th. This could relate to family or friends and could even spill over into the area of your offspring around the 21st. Try to clarify any misunderstandings and you mustn't allow scrambled rushing for Christmas shopping to faze you.

Your morning regime will need a pick-me-up after the madness of the festive season, so around the 28th and 29th, get stuck into your vitamins, recommit to your plan to improve your health and vitality and, of course, if you've had a little bit too much to drink, don't let your brittle state of mind cause you to be impolite.

An off-beat contrast is what is needed around the 30th when the Moon moves into your ninth house and also reconnects with Venus, the planet of love, on the 31st. If you've been feeling a little unnoticed you may need to retrain yourself in the art of seduction. But, by the same token, a letter of interest will prompt you to use your grooviest keystrokes to respond to a last-minute romantic enquiry. This is a nice way to top off 2010, irrespective of how fatigued you may feel from the Christmas experience.

Work and money

A telephone questionnaire or marketing scam is definitely out of the question on the 3rd, particularly if it's from an unwanted, outsourced location somewhere in China or Mexico! Here's an idea: when you answer the phone and they ask, 'are you the owner of the business?', simply tell them to hang onto the line and never answer it again.

'Eat, drink and be merry' seems to be your mood around the 7th, but don't overdo it. It's not a bad idea to get closer to someone who has more experience in the job, so do ask for their help. You will be surprised at how willing people are to give you a hand, especially when they see you struggling with a deadline.

A brilliant business idea may need to come under the heading of an 'abridged venture' and this will be the case if you don't quite have the funds or the support of those who count. To begin with, shrink the idea down to a manageable size. During the period of the 9th till the 12th it's probably better for you to focus your attention on social and family matters rather than try to kick-start an independent business scheme. There's plenty of time for that in the new year.

With Christmas around the corner, remember that banks are not philanthropic institutions. You'll need to have all your paperwork together around the 17th if you want a bit of extra cash, an extra credit card or an advance or overdraft for your business.

A thankless, phoney clerk or sales assistant is the last thing you need, but may have to deal with, around the 23rd or the 24th. Just get it over and done with and don't invest too much mental and emotional energy in something that has become part and parcel of the Christmas season.

Destiny dates

Positive: 7, 8, 9, 14, 31
Negative: 3, 19, 21, 23, 24
Mixed: 10, 11, 12, 13, 17, 28, 29, 30

2010:
Astronumerology

The greatest discovery of my generation is that
human beings can alter their lives by altering
their attitudes of mind.

—William James

The power behind your name

By adding the numbers of your name you can see
which planet is ruling you. Each of the letters of
the alphabet is assigned a number, which is listed
below. These numbers are ruled by the planets.
This is according to the ancient Chaldean system of
numerology and is very different to the Pythagorean
system to which many refer.

Each number is assigned a planet:

AIQJY	=	1	**Sun**
BKR	=	2	**Moon**
CGLS	=	3	**Jupiter**
DMT	=	4	**Uranus**
EHNX	=	5	**Mercury**
UVW	=	6	**Venus**
OZ	=	7	**Neptune**
FP	=	8	**Saturn**
—	=	9	**Mars**

Notice that the number 9 is not aligned with a letter
because it is considered special. Once the numbers
have been added you will see that a single planet

rules your name and personal affairs. Many famous actors, writers and musicians change their names to attract the energy of a luckier planet. You can experiment with the list and try new names or add the letters of your second name to see how that vibration suits you. It's a lot of fun!

Here is an example of how to find out the power of your name. If your name is John Smith, calculate the ruling planet by assigning each letter to a number in the table like this:

J O H N S M I T H
1 7 5 5 3 4 1 4 5

Now add the numbers like this:
1 + 7 + 5 + 5 + 3 + 4 + 1 + 4 + 5 = 35
Then add 3 + 5 = 8

The ruling number of John Smith's name is 8, which is ruled by Saturn. Now study the name-number table to reveal the power of your name. The numbers 3 and 5 will also play a secondary role in John's character and destiny, so in this case you would also study the effects of Jupiter and Mercury.

Name-number table

Your name number	Ruling planet	Your name characteristics
1	**Sun**	Magnetic individual. Great energy and life force. Physically dynamic and sociable. Attracts good friends and individuals in powerful positions. Good government connections. Intelligent, impressive, flashy and victorious. A loyal number for relationships.
2	**Moon**	Soft, emotional nature. Changeable moods but psychic, intuitive senses. Imaginative nature and empathetic expression of feelings. Loves family, mother and home life. Night owl who probably needs more sleep. Success with the public and/or women.
3	**Jupiter**	Outgoing, optimistic number with lucky overtones. Attracts opportunities without trying. Good sense of timing. Religious or spiritual aspirations.

Your name number	Ruling planet	Your name characteristics
		Can investigate the meaning of life. Loves to travel and explore the world and people.
4	Uranus	Explosive character with many unusual aspects. Likes the untried and novel. Forward thinking, with many extra-ordinary friends. Gets fed up easily so needs plenty of invigorating experiences. Pioneering, technological and imaginative. Wilful and stubborn when wants to be. Unexpected events in life may be positive or negative.
5	Mercury	Quick-thinking mind with great powers of speech. Extremely vigorous life; always on the go and lives on nervous energy. Youthful attitude and never grows old. Looks younger than actual age. Young friends and humorous disposition. Loves reading and writing.
6	Venus	Delightful personality. Graceful and attractive character who cherishes friends

Your name number	Ruling planet	Your name characteristics
		and social life. Musical or artistic interests. Good for money making as well as abundant love affairs. Career in the public eye is possible. Loves family but is often overly concerned by friends.
7	Neptune	Intuitive, spiritual and self-sacrificing nature. Easily misled by those who need help. Loves to dream of life's possibilities. Has curative powers. Dreams are revealing and prophetic. Loves the water and will have many journeys in life. Spiritual aspirations dominate worldly desires.
8	Saturn	Hard-working, focused individual with slow but certain success. Incredible concentration and self-sacrifice for a goal.
		Money orientated but generous when trust is gained. Professional but may be a hard taskmaster. Demands

		highest standards and needs to learn to enjoy life a little more.
9	**Mars**	Fantastic physical drive and ambition. Sports and outdoor activities are keys to wellbeing. Confrontational. Likes to work and play just as hard. Caring and protective of family, friends and territory. Individual tastes in life but is also self-absorbed. Needs to listen to others' advice to gain greater success.

Your 2010 planetary ruler

Astrology and numerology are very intimately connected. As already shown, each planet rules over a number between 1 and 9. Both your name *and* your birth date are ruled by planetary energies.

Add the numbers of your birth date and the year in question to find out which planet will control the coming year for you.

For example, if you were born on the 12th of November, add the numerals 1 and 2 (12, your day of birth) and 1 and 1 (11, your month of birth) to the year in question, in this case 2010 (the current year), like this:

$$1 + 2 + 1 + 1 + 2 + 0 + 1 + 0 = 8$$

The planet ruling your individual karma for 2010 will be Saturn because this planet rules the number 8.

You can even take your ruling name-number as shown earlier and add it to the year in question to throw more light on your coming personal affairs, like this:

John Smith = 8

Year coming = 2010

8 + 2 + 0 + 1 + 0 = 11

1 + 1 = 2

Therefore, 2 is the ruling number of the combined name and date vibrations. Study the Moon's number 2 influence for 2010.

Outlines of the year number ruled by each planet are given below. Enjoy!

1 is the year of the Sun

Overview

The Sun is the brightest object in the heavens and rules number 1 and the sign of Leo. Because of this the coming year will bring you great success and popularity.

You'll be full of life and radiant vibrations and are more than ready to tackle your new nine-year cycle, which begins now. Any new projects you commence are likely to be successful.

Your health and vitality will be very strong and your stamina at its peak. Even if you happen to have the odd problem with your health, your recuperative power will be strong.

You have tremendous magnetism this year so social popularity won't be a problem for you. I see many new friends and lovers coming into your life. Expect loads of invitations to parties and fun-filled outings. Just don't take your health for granted as you're likely to burn the candle at both ends.

With success coming your way, don't let it go to your head. You must maintain humility, which will make you even more popular in the coming year.

Love and pleasure

This is an important cycle for renewing your love and connections with your family, particularly if you have children. The Sun is connected with the sign of Leo and therefore brings an increase in musical and theatrical activities. Entertainment and other creative hobbies will be high on your agenda and bring you a great sense of satisfaction.

Work

You won't have to make too much of an effort to be successful this year because the brightness of the Sun will draw opportunities to you. Changes in work are likely and, if you have been concerned that opportunities are few and far between, 2010 will be different. You can expect some sort of promotion or an increase in income because your employers will take special note of your skills and service orientation.

Improving your luck

Leo is the ruler of number 1 and, therefore, if you're born under this star sign, 2010 will be particularly lucky. For others, July and August, the months of Leo, will bring good fortune. The 1st, 8th, 15th and 22nd hours of Sundays especially will give you a unique sort of luck in any sort of competition or activities generally. Keep your eye out for those born under Leo as they may be able to contribute something to your life and may even have a karmic connection to you. This is a particularly important year for your destiny.

Your lucky numbers in this coming cycle are 1, 10, 19 and 28.

2 is the year of the Moon

Overview

There's nothing more soothing than the cool light of the full Moon on a clear night. The Moon is emotional and receptive and controls your destiny in 2010. If you're able to use the positive energies of the Moon, it will be a great year in which you can realign and improve your relationships, particularly with family members.

Making a commitment to becoming a better person and bringing your emotions under control will also dominate your thinking. Try not to let your emotions get the better of you throughout the coming year because you may be drawn into the changeable nature of these lunar vibrations as well. If you fail to keep control of your emotional life you'll later regret some of your actions. You must blend careful thinking with feeling to arrive at the best results. Your luck throughout 2010 will certainly be determined by the state of your mind.

Because the Moon and the sign of Cancer rule the number 2 there is a certain amount of change to be expected this year. Keep your feelings steady and don't let your heart rule your head.

Love and pleasure

Your primary concern in 2010 will be your home and family life. You'll be finally keen to take on those renovations, or work on your garden. You may even think of buying a new home. You can at last carry out some of those plans and make your dreams come true. If you find yourself a little more temperamental than usual, do some extra meditation and spend time alone until you sort this out. You mustn't withhold your feelings from your partner as this will only create frustration.

Work

During 2010 your focus will be primarily on feelings and family; however, this doesn't mean you can't make great strides in your work as well. The Moon rules the general public and what you might find is that special opportunities and connections with the world at large present themselves to you. You could be working with large numbers of people.

If you're looking for a better work opportunity, try to focus your attention on women who can give you a hand. Use your intuition as it will be finely tuned this year. Work and career success depends upon your instincts.

Improving your luck

The sign of Cancer is your ruler this year and because the Moon rules Mondays, both this day of the week and the month of July are extremely lucky for you. The 1st, 8th, 15th and 22nd hours on Mondays will be very powerful. Pay special attention to the new and full Moon days throughout 2010.

The numbers 2, 11 and 29 are lucky for you.

3 is the year of Jupiter

Overview

The year 2010 will be a number 3 year for you and, because of this, Jupiter and Sagittarius will dominate your affairs. This is extremely lucky and shows you'll be motivated to broaden your horizons, gain more money and become extremely popular in your social circles. It looks like 2010 will be a fun-filled year with much excitement.

Jupiter and Sagittarius are generous to a fault and so, likewise, your open-handedness will mark the year. You'll be friendly and helpful to all of those around you.

Pisces is also under the rulership of the number 3 and this brings out your spiritual and compassion-ate nature. You'll become a much better person, reducing your negative karma by increasing your self-awareness and spiritual feelings. You will want to share your luck with those you love.

Love and pleasure

Travel and seeking new adventures will be part and parcel of your romantic life this year. Travelling to distant lands and meeting unusual people will open your heart to fresh possibilities of romance.

You'll try novel and audacious things and will find yourself in a different circle of friends. Compromise will be important in making your existing relationships work. Talk about your feelings. If you are currently in a relationship you'll feel an upswing in your affection for your partner. This is a perfect opportunity to deepen your love for each other and take your relationship to a new level.

If you're not yet attached to someone, there's good news for you. Great opportunities lie in store and a spiritual or karmic connection may be experienced in 2010.

Work

Great fortune can be expected through your working life in the next twelve months. Your friends and work colleagues will want to help you achieve your goals. Even your employers will be amenable to your requests for extra money or a better position within the organisation.

If you want to start a new job or possibly begin an independent line of business, this is a great year to do it. Jupiter looks set to give you plenty of opportunities, success and a superior reputation.

Improving your luck

As long as you can keep a balanced view of things and not overdo anything, your luck will increase dramatically throughout 2010. The important thing is to remain grounded and not be too airy-fairy about your objectives. Be realistic about your talents and capabilities and don't brag about your skills or achievements. This will only invite envy from others.

Moderate your social life as well and don't drink or eat too much as this will slow your reflexes and weaken your chances for success.

You have plenty of spiritual insights this year so you should use them to their maximum. In the 1st, 8th, 15th and 24th hours of Thursdays you should use your intuition to enhance your luck, and the numbers 3, 12, 21 and 30 are also lucky for you. March and December are your lucky months but generally the whole year should go pretty smoothly for you.

4 is the year of Uranus

Overview

The electric and exciting planet of the zodiac, Uranus, and its sign of Aquarius, rule your affairs throughout 2010. Dramatic events will surprise and at the same time unnerve you in your professional and personal life. So be prepared!

You'll be able to achieve many things this year and your dreams are likely to come true, but you mustn't be distracted or scattered with your energies. You'll be breaking through your own self-limitations and this will present challenges from your family and friends. You'll want to be independent and develop your spiritual powers and nothing will stop you.

Try to maintain discipline and an orderly lifestyle so you can make the most of these special energies this year. If unexpected things do happen, it's not a bad idea to have an alternative plan so you don't lose momentum.

Love and pleasure

You want something radical, something different in your relationships this year. It's quite likely that your love life will be feeling a little less than exciting so you'll take some important steps to change that. If your partner is as progressive as you'll be this year, then your relationship is likely to improve and fulfil both of you.

In your social life you will meet some very unusual people, whom you'll feel are especially connected to you spiritually. You may want to ditch everything for the excitement and passion of a completely new relationship, but tread carefully as this may not work out exactly as you expect it to.

Work

Technology, computing and the Internet will play a larger role in your professional life this coming year.

You'll have to move ahead with the times and learn new skills if you want to achieve success.

A hectic schedule is likely, so make sure your diary is with you at all times. Try to be more efficient and don't waste time.

New friends and alliances at work will help you achieve even greater success in the coming period. Becoming a team player will be even more important in gaining satisfaction from your professional endeavours.

Improving your luck

Moving too quickly and impulsively will cause you problems on all fronts, so be a little more patient and think your decisions through more carefully. Social, romantic and professional opportunities will come to you but take a little time to investigate the ramifications of your actions.

The 1st, 8th, 15th and 20th hours of any Saturday are lucky, but love and luck are likely to cross your path when you least expect it. The numbers 4, 13, 22 and 31 are also lucky for you this year.

5 is the year of Mercury

Overview

The supreme planet of communication, Mercury, is your ruling planet throughout 2010. The number 5, which is connected to Mercury, will confer upon you success through your intellectual abilities.

Any form of writing or speaking will be improved and this will be, to a large extent, underpinning your success. Your imagination will be stimulated by this planet, with many incredible new and exciting ideas coming to mind.

Mercury and the number 5 are considered somewhat indecisive. Be firm in your attitude and don't let too many ideas or opportunities distract and confuse you. By all means get as much information as you can to help you make the right decisions.

I see you involved with money proposals, job applications, even contracts that need to be signed, so remain as clear-headed as possible.

Your business skills and clear and concise communication will be at the heart of your life in 2010.

Love and pleasure

Mercury, which rules the signs of Gemini and Virgo, will make your love life a little difficult due to its changeable nature. On the one hand you'll feel passionate and loving to your partner, yet on the other you will feel like giving it all up for the excitement of a new affair. Maintain the middle ground.

Also, try not to be too critical with your friends and family members. The influence of Virgo makes you prone to expecting much more from others than they're capable of giving. Control your sharp tongue and don't hurt people's feelings. Encouraging others is the better path, leading to greater emotional satisfaction.

Work

Speed will dominate your professional life in 2010. You'll be flitting from one subject to another and taking on far more than you can handle. You'll need to make some serious changes in your routine to handle the avalanche of work that will come your way. You'll also be travelling with your work, but not necessarily overseas.

If you're in a job you enjoy then this year will give you additional successes. If not, it may be time to move on.

Improving your luck

Communication is the key to attaining your desires in the coming twelve months. Keep focused on one idea rather than scattering your energies in all directions and your success will be speedier.

By looking after your health, sleeping well and exercising regularly, you'll build up your resilience and mental strength.

The 1st, 8th, 15th and 20th hours of Wednesday are lucky so it's best to schedule your meetings and other important social engagements during these times. The lucky numbers for Mercury are 5, 14, 23 and 32.

6 is the year of Venus

Overview

Because you're ruled by 6 this year, love is in the air! Venus, Taurus and Libra are well known for their affinity with romance, love, and even marriage. If ever you were going to meet a soulmate and feel comfortable in love, 2010 must surely be your year.

Taurus has a strong connection to money and practical affairs as well, so finances will also improve if you are diligent about work and security issues.

The important thing to keep in mind this year is that sharing love and making that important soul connection should be kept high on your agenda. This will be an enjoyable period in your life.

Love and pleasure

Romance is the key thing for you this year and your current relationships will become more fulfilling if you happen to be attached. For singles, a 6 year heralds an important meeting that eventually leads to marriage.

You'll also be interested in fashion, gifts, jewellery and all sorts of socialising. It's at one of these social engagements that you could meet the love of your life. Remain available!

Venus is one of the planets that has a tendency to overdo things, so be moderate in your eating and drinking. Try generally to maintain a modest lifestyle.

Work

You'll have a clearer insight into finances and your future security during a number 6 year. Whereas previously you may have had additional expenses and extra distractions, your mind will now be more settled and capable of longer-term planning along these lines.

With the extra cash you might see this year, decorating your home or office will give you a special sort of satisfaction.

Social affairs and professional activities will be strongly linked. Any sort of work-related functions may offer you romantic opportunities as well. On the other hand, be careful not to mix up your work-place relationships with romantic ideals. This could complicate some of your professional activities.

Improving your luck

You'll want more money and a life of leisure and ease in 2010. Keep working on your strengths and eliminate your negative personality traits to create greater luck and harmony in your life.

Moderate all your actions and don't focus exclusively on money and material objects. Feed your spiritual needs as well. By balancing your inner and outer sides you'll see that your romantic and professional lives will be enhanced more easily.

The 1st, 8th, 15th and 20th hours on Fridays will be very lucky for you and new opportunities will arise for you at those times. You can use the numbers 6, 15, 24 and 33 to increase luck in your general affairs.

7 is the year of Neptune

Overview

The last and most evolved sign of the zodiac is

Pisces, which is ruled by Neptune. The number 7 is deeply connected with this zodiac sign and governs you in 2010. Your ideals seem to be clearer and more spiritually orientated than ever before. Your desire to evolve and understand your inner self will be a double-edged sword. It depends on how organised you are as to how well you can use these spiritual and abstract concepts in your practical life.

Your past hurts and deep emotional issues will be dealt with and removed for good, if you are serious about becoming a better human being.

Spend a little more time caring for yourself rather than others, as it's likely some of your friends will drain you of energy with their own personal problems. Of course, you mustn't turn a blind eye to the needs of others, but don't ignore your own personal requirements in the process.

Love and pleasure

Meeting people with similar life views and spiritual aspirations will rekindle your faith in relationships. If you do choose to develop a new romance, make sure there is a clear understanding of the responsibilities of one to the other. Don't get swept off your feet by people who have ulterior motives.

Keep your relationships realistic and see that the most idealistic partnerships must eventually come down to Earth. Deal with the practicalities of life.

Work

This is a year of hard work, but one in which you'll

come to understand the deeper significance of your professional ideals. You may discover a whole new aspect to your career, which involves a more compassionate and self-sacrificing side to your personality.

You'll also find that your way of working will change and you'll be more focused and able to get into the spirit of whatever you do. Finding meaningful work is very likely and therefore this could be a year when money, security, creativity and spirituality overlap to bring you a great sense of personal satisfaction.

Tapping into your greater self through meditation and self-study will bring you great benefits throughout 2010.

Improving your luck

Using self-sacrifice along with discrimination will be an unusual method of improving your luck. The laws of karma state that what you give, you receive in greater measure. This is one of the principal themes for you in 2010.

The 1st, 8th, 15th and 20th hours of Tuesdays are your lucky times. The numbers 7, 16, 25 and 34 should be used to increase your lucky energies.

8 is the year of Saturn

Overview

The earthy and practical sign of Capricorn and its ruler Saturn are intimately linked to the number

8, which rules you in 2010. Your discipline and far-sightedness will help you achieve great things in the coming year. With cautious discernment, slowly but surely you will reach your goals.

It may be that due to the influence of the solitary Saturn, your best work and achievement will be behind closed doors away from the limelight. You mustn't fear this as you'll discover many new things about yourself. You'll learn just how strong you really are.

Love and pleasure

Work will overshadow your personal affairs in 2010, but you mustn't let this erode the personal relationships you have. Becoming a workaholic brings great material successes but will also cause you to become too insular and aloof. Your family members won't take too kindly to you working 100-hour weeks.

Responsibility is one of the key words for this number and you will therefore find yourself in a position of authority that leaves very little time for fun. Try to make the time to enjoy the company of friends and family and by all means schedule time off on the weekends as it will give you the peace of mind you're looking for.

Because of your responsible attitude it will be very hard for you not to assume a greater role in your workplace and this indicates longer working hours with the likelihood of a promotion with equally good remuneration.

Work

Money is high on your agenda in 2010. Number 8 is a good money number according to the Chinese and this year is at last likely to bring you the fruits of your hard labour. You are cautious and resourceful in all your dealings and will not waste your hard-earned savings. You will also be very conscious of using your time wisely.

You will be given more responsibilities and you're likely to take them on, if only to prove to yourself that you can handle whatever life dishes up.

Expect a promotion in which you'll play a leading role in your work. Your diligence and hard work will pay off, literally, in a bigger salary and more respect from others.

Improving your luck

Caution is one of the key characteristics of the number 8 and is linked to Capricorn. But being overly cautious could cause you to miss valuable opportunities. If an offer is put to you, try to think outside the square and balance it with your naturally cautious nature.

Be gentle and kind to yourself. By loving yourself, others will naturally love you, too. The 1st, 8th, 15th and 20th hours of Saturdays are exceptionally lucky for you, as are the numbers 1, 8, 17, 26 and 35.

9 is the year of Mars

Overview

You are now entering the final year of a nine-year cycle dominated by the planet Mars and the sign of Aries. You'll be completing many things and are determined to be successful after several years of intense work.

Some of your relationships may now have reached their use-by date and even personal affairs may need to be released. Don't let arguments and disagreements get in the road of friendly resolution in these areas of your life.

Mars is a challenging planet, and this year, although you will be very active and productive, you may find others trying to obstruct the achievement of your goals. As a result you may react strongly to them, thereby creating disharmony in your workplace. Don't be so impulsive or reckless, and generally slow things down. The slower, steadier approach has greater merit this year.

Love and pleasure

If you become too bossy and pushy with friends this year you will just end up pushing them out of your life. It's a year to end certain friendships but by the same token it could be the perfect time to remove conflicts and thereby bolster your love affairs in 2010.

If you're feeling a little irritable and angry with those you love, try getting rid of these negative feelings through some intense, rigorous sports and physical activity. This will definitely relieve tension and improve your personal life.

Work

Because you're healthy and able to work at a more intense pace you'll achieve an incredible amount in the coming year. Overwork could become a problem if you're not careful.

Because the number 9 and Mars are infused with leadership energy, you'll be asked to take the reins of the job and steer your company or group in a certain direction. This will bring with it added responsibility but also a greater sense of purpose for you.

Improving your luck

Because of the hot and restless energy of the number 9, it is important to create more mental peace in your life this year. Lower the temperature, so to speak, and decompress your relationships rather than becoming aggravated. Try to talk with your work partners and loved ones rather than telling them what to do. This will generally pick up your health and your relationships.

The 1st, 8th, 15th and 20th hours of Tuesdays are the luckiest for you this year and, if you're involved in any disputes or need to attend to health issues, these times are also very good to get the best results. Your lucky numbers are 9, 18, 27 and 36.

PISCES

2010:
Your Daily Planner

*If you will call your troubles 'experiences'—and
remember that every experience develops some latent
force within you—you will grow vigorous and happy,
however adverse your circumstances may seem to be.*

—James Russell Miller

According to astrology, the success of any venture or
activity is dependent upon the planetary positions
at the time you commence that activity. Electional
astrology helps you select the most appropriate
times for many of your day-to-day endeavours.
These dates are applicable to each and every zodiac
sign and can be used freely by one and all, even if
your star sign doesn't fall under the one mentioned
in this book. Please note that the daily planner is a
universal system applicable equally to all *twelve* star
signs. Anyone and everyone can use this planner
irrespective of their birth sign.

Ancient astrologers understood the planetary
patterns and how they impacted on each of us. This
allowed them to suggest the best possible times
to start various important activities. For example,
many farmers still use this approach today: they
understand the phases of the Moon, and attest to
the fact that planting seeds on certain lunar days
produces a far better crop than does planting on
other days.

In the following section, many facets of daily
life are considered. Using the lunar cycle and the
combined strength of other planets allows us to
work out the best times to do them. This is your

personal almanac, which can be used in conjunction with any star sign to help optimise the results.

First, select the activity you are interested in, and then quickly scan the year for the best months to start it. When you have selected the month, you can finetune your timing by finding the best specific dates. You can then be sure that the planetary energies will be in sync with you, offering you the best possible outcome.

Coupled with what you know about your monthly and weekly trends, the daily planner is an effective tool to help you capitalise on opportunities that come your way this year.

Good luck, and may the planets bless you with great success, fortune and happiness in 2010!

Getting started in 2010

How many times have you made a new year's resolution to begin a diet or be a better person in your relationships? And, how many times has it not worked out? Well, part of the reason may be that you started out at the wrong time, because how successful you are is strongly influenced by the position of the Moon and the planets when you begin a particular activity. You will be more successful with the following endeavours if you start them on the days indicated.

Relationships

We all feel more empowered on some days than on others. This is because the planets have some power over us—their movement and their relationships to each other determine the ebb and flow of our energies. And, our levels of self-confidence and sense of romantic magnetism play an important part in the way we behave in relationships.

Your daily planner tells you the ideal dates for meeting new friends, initiating a love affair, spending time with family and loved ones—it even tells you the most appropriate times for sexual encounters.

You'll be surprised at how much more impact you will make in your relationships when you tune yourself in to the planetary energies on these special dates.

Falling in love/restoring love

During these times you could expect favourable energies to meet your soulmate or, if you've had difficulty in a relationship, to approach the one you love to rekindle both your and their emotional responses:

January	18, 20, 23, 24
February	15, 16, 20, 24
March	29
April	16
May	14, 17, 18, 19, 20, 23
June	14, 15, 16, 20, 21
July	12
August	10, 13, 14
September	9, 21, 22
October	8, 18, 19, 20

November	14, 15, 16, 19, 20, 21
December	13, 17, 18

Special times with friends and family

Socialising, partying and having a good time with those whose company you enjoy is highly favourable under the following dates. They are excellent to spend time with family and loved ones in a domestic environment:

January	6, 26, 27
February	12, 13, 14, 15, 16, 20, 24
March	11, 21, 22, 29, 30, 31
April	8
May	15, 16, 17, 18, 19, 20, 23, 24
June	1, 2, 3, 11, 12, 14, 15, 16, 20, 21, 29, 30
July	8, 9, 12, 17, 18, 26, 27
August	5, 6, 9, 10, 13, 14, 22, 23, 24
September	1, 2, 5, 9, 10, 18, 19, 20, 30
October	3, 19, 20, 25, 26, 30, 31
November	3, 4, 14, 15, 16, 22, 26, 27
December	2, 9, 10, 11, 19, 20, 24, 25

Healing or resuming relationships

If you're trying to get back together with the one you love or need a heart-to-heart or deep-and-meaningful discussion with someone, you can try the following dates to do so:

January	12, 13, 14, 15, 21, 22, 23, 24, 25
February	6

March	6, 31
April	2, 7, 8, 12, 16, 19, 23, 24, 25, 26
May	10, 11, 12, 13, 14, 15, 16, 17, 18, 19, 20, 21, 22, 23, 24, 25, 26, 27, 28, 30
June	3, 8, 9, 10, 11, 12, 13, 14, 15, 16, 17, 21, 22, 23, 25, 26, 27, 28, 29, 30
July	1, 2, 3, 4, 5, 10, 11, 12, 13, 15, 16, 17, 18, 19, 20, 21, 22, 23, 28, 29, 30
August	1, 2, 3, 4, 5, 6, 9, 10, 13, 14, 15, 16, 20, 23, 25, 26, 27
September	2, 5, 9, 10, 13, 17, 18, 19, 20
October	1, 2, 3, 6, 12, 13, 14, 15, 20, 22, 23, 24, 25, 26, 27, 28, 29, 30, 31
November	3, 4, 5, 6, 7, 8, 9, 21, 27, 28, 29, 30
December	2, 3, 4, 6, 12, 13, 14, 17, 18, 19, 20, 21, 23, 24, 25

Sexual encounters

Physical and sexual energies are well favoured on the following dates. The energies of the planets enhance your moments of intimacy during these times:

January	1, 6, 7, 21, 22
February	6, 12, 13, 14, 20, 24
March	14, 15, 17, 18, 19, 30, 31
April	23, 24, 25, 26
May	9, 12, 14, 17, 18, 19, 20
June	3, 8, 9, 10, 11, 14, 15, 16, 20, 21, 29, 30

July	8, 9, 10, 11, 12
August	6, 10, 13, 14, 22, 23, 24
September	3, 4, 5, 6, 9, 10, 18, 19, 20, 21, 22, 30
October	1, 2, 3, 7, 8, 18, 19, 20, 23, 24, 28, 29, 30, 31
November	3, 4, 14, 15, 16, 19, 24, 25, 26, 27
December	2, 10, 11, 12, 13, 15, 16, 17, 19, 20, 22, 23, 24, 25

Health and wellbeing

Your aura and life force are susceptible to the movements of the planets—in particular, they respond to the phases of the Moon.

The following dates are the most appropriate times to begin a diet, have cosmetic surgery, or seek medical advice. They also indicate the best times to help others.

Feeling of wellbeing

Your physical as well as your mental alertness should be strong on these following dates. You can plan your activities and expect a good response from others:

January	2, 3, 4, 5, 6, 7, 11, 12, 13, 14, 16, 17, 18, 21, 22, 23, 24, 30, 31
February	1, 2, 7, 8, 15, 16, 17, 18, 19, 20, 21, 22, 23, 24, 25, 26, 27, 28
March	16, 17, 18, 19, 20, 22, 23, 24, 25, 26, 27, 28, 29
April	7, 13, 14, 16, 28

May	2, 11, 14, 25, 26
June	8, 22, 23, 26, 27, 28, 29, 30
July	4, 5, 8, 9, 12, 13, 14, 15, 16, 19, 20, 23, 24, 25
August	5, 6, 9, 10, 11, 12, 13, 15, 16, 20, 21
September	9, 10, 11, 12, 13, 16, 17, 21, 22, 24, 25, 28, 29, 30
October	3, 4, 5, 6, 7, 8, 9, 10, 13, 14, 15, 22
November	4, 5, 6, 10, 11, 19, 20, 21
December	7, 8, 17, 18, 28, 29

Healing and medicine

These times are good for approaching others who have expertise when you need some deeper understanding. They are also favourable for any sort of healing or medication and making appointments with doctors or psychologists. Planning surgery around these dates should bring good results.

Often giving up our time and energy to assist others doesn't necessarily result in the expected outcome. However, by lending a helping hand to a friend on the following dates, the results should be favourable:

January	1, 2, 3, 4, 6, 7, 8, 9, 11, 12, 13, 14, 15, 16, 17, 18, 19, 20, 21, 22, 23, 24, 26, 27, 28, 29, 30, 31
February	1, 5, 6, 9, 11, 12, 13, 14, 15, 16, 19
March	1, 2, 3, 4, 5, 8, 9, 10, 11, 12, 18, 19, 24, 25, 29

April	1, 3, 4, 5, 22, 26
May	4, 5
June	1, 2, 3, 9, 10, 17, 18, 22, 23, 24, 25, 29, 30
July	6, 7, 15, 16, 17, 18, 19, 21, 22, 23, 24, 25, 26
August	2, 3, 4, 11, 12, 17, 18, 19, 20, 21, 30, 31
September	6, 7, 8, 10, 11, 12, 13, 14, 15, 16, 17, 18, 26, 27, 28, 29
October	5, 7, 8, 9, 10, 11, 12, 13, 14, 15, 16, 17, 18, 19, 20, 21, 22, 23, 24, 25, 26, 28, 29, 30, 31
November	1, 2, 3, 5, 7, 8, 10, 11, 14, 15, 17, 18, 19, 22, 23
December	4, 5, 7, 8, 9, 10, 12, 13, 14, 16, 23, 24, 25, 26, 28, 29, 30, 31

Money

Money is an important part of life, and involves many decisions—decisions about borrowing, investing, spending. The ideal times for transactions are very much influenced by the planets, and whether your investment or nest egg grows or doesn't grow can often be linked to timing. Making your decisions on the following dates could give you a whole new perspective on your financial future.

Managing wealth and money

To build your nest egg it's a good time to open your bank account or invest money on the following dates:

January   1, 6, 7, 13, 14, 15, 18, 21, 22, 28, 29

178

February	3, 4, 9, 10, 11, 12, 13, 14, 15, 17, 18, 24, 25
March	2, 3, 9, 10, 16, 17, 18, 23, 24, 29, 30, 31
April	5, 6, 7, 13, 14, 19, 20, 21, 26, 27,
May	2, 3, 4, 10, 11, 17, 18, 23, 24, 30, 31
June	6, 7, 8, 13, 14, 19, 20, 21, 26, 27, 28
July	4, 5, 10, 11, 12, 17, 18, 23, 24, 25, 31
August	1, 7, 8, 13, 14, 20, 21, 27, 28, 29
September	3, 4, 9, 10, 16, 17, 23, 24, 25
October	1, 2, 7, 8, 13, 14, 15, 21, 22, 28, 29
November	3, 4, 10, 11, 17, 18, 24, 25
December	1, 2, 7, 8, 14, 15, 16, 21, 22, 23, 24, 29

Spending

It's always fun to spend but the following dates are more in tune with this activity and are likely to give you better results:

January	3, 4, 5, 6, 7, 8, 9, 10, 11, 12, 13, 14
February	3, 4, 5, 10, 19
March	8, 10, 11, 13, 14, 19
April	7, 8, 11, 12, 22
May	6, 7, 8, 9, 10, 11, 12, 13, 17, 18, 19, 20, 21, 22, 23, 24, 25, 26, 27, 28
June	1, 11, 12, 14, 16, 17, 19, 23, 25, 26, 27, 28, 29, 30
July	6, 7, 8, 23, 24, 25, 26, 27, 28, 29, 31
August	1, 2, 3, 4, 5, 15, 16, 17, 18, 19, 30, 31
September	1, 2, 3, 4, 17, 18, 19, 20, 21, 22, 23, 27, 28, 29, 30

October	4, 7, 12, 13, 14, 15, 16, 17, 18, 19, 27, 28
November	2, 3, 4, 25, 26, 27, 28
December	11, 22, 23

Selling

If you're thinking of selling something, whether it is small or large, consider the following dates as ideal times to do so:

January	18
February	12, 13, 14, 15
March	5, 6, 9, 14, 15, 16, 17, 18, 19, 21
April	1, 3, 4, 5, 22, 26
May	7, 12, 21, 29
June	3, 8, 9, 10, 11, 12, 13, 17, 24, 25, 26, 27, 28, 30
July	1, 2, 7, 9, 10, 11, 25, 27, 28, 29, 30, 31
August	1, 2, 3, 4, 5, 6, 7, 8, 9, 10, 13, 20, 23, 28
September	2, 9, 10, 11, 12, 13, 14, 15, 16, 17, 18, 19, 20, 21, 22, 23, 24, 26, 30
October	1, 2, 3, 4, 6, 7, 10, 11, 17, 18, 19, 20, 21, 22, 23, 24, 25, 27, 29
November	3, 4, 5, 6, 7, 11, 14, 15, 16, 17, 18, 19, 21, 23, 24, 25, 26, 27, 28, 29, 30
December	1, 2, 3, 4, 5, 6, 7, 8, 9, 10, 11, 12, 13, 14, 15, 16, 17, 18, 19, 20, 21, 22

Borrowing

Few of us like to borrow money, but if you must, taking out a loan on the following dates will be positive:

January	12, 30
February	7, 12, 13
March	6, 7, 8, 11
April	3, 4, 8
May	9, 28, 29
June	1, 2, 3, 4, 5, 29, 30
July	1, 2, 3, 26, 27, 28, 29, 30
August	9, 25, 26
September	5, 6
October	3, 30
November	26, 27
December	3, 4, 21, 22, 23, 30, 31

Work and education

Your career is important, and continual improvement of your skills is therefore also crucial professionally, mentally and socially. The dates below will help you find out the most appropriate times to improve your professional talents and commence new work or education associated with your work.

You may need to decide when to start learning a new skill, when to ask for a promotion, and even when to make an important career change. Here are the days when your mental and educational power is strong.

Learning new skills

Educational pursuits are lucky and bring good results on the following dates:

January	15, 16, 17, 18, 19, 20, 21, 22, 25, 26, 27
February	14, 15, 16, 17, 18, 19, 22, 23, 28
March	16, 17, 18, 21, 22, 27, 28
April	17, 18, 24, 25
May	15, 16, 21, 22
June	12, 17, 18, 24, 25
July	15, 16, 21, 22, 23, 24, 25
August	11, 12, 17, 18, 19
September	8, 13, 15, 20, 21, 22
October	11, 12
November	7, 8, 9
December	6, 19, 20

Changing career path or profession

If you're feeling stuck and need to move into a new professional activity, changing jobs could be done at these times:

January	6, 7, 15, 16, 17, 23, 24
February	12, 13, 14, 19, 20, 21
March	19, 20, 27, 28
April	15, 16, 24, 25
May	14, 21, 22
June	17, 18, 19, 20, 21
July	8, 9, 15, 16, 23, 24, 25

August	5, 6, 11, 12, 20, 21, 22, 23
September	1, 2, 8, 13, 14, 15, 17
October	8, 13, 14, 15, 16, 17
November	3, 4, 10, 11, 19, 20, 21
December	1, 2, 3, 7, 8, 17, 18, 28, 29

Promotion, professional focus and hard work

To increase your mental focus and achieve good results from the work you do; promotions are also likely on these dates:

January	4, 5, 6, 11, 12, 13, 14, 15, 16, 17, 18, 19, 21
February	6
March	16, 17, 18, 19, 20, 21, 23, 24, 25, 26, 27, 28, 29
April	8, 28, 29
May	12, 21
June	25, 26, 27, 28
July	4, 5, 8, 9, 12, 13, 14, 15, 16, 17, 18, 19, 20, 21, 22, 23, 24, 25, 26, 27
August	5, 6, 10, 11, 12, 13, 14, 15, 16, 17, 18, 19, 20, 21, 22, 23, 24
September	13, 14, 15
October	10, 11, 12, 13, 14, 15, 17, 18, 19, 20, 22, 23, 24, 30, 31
November	2, 4, 5, 6, 7, 8, 9, 23, 24, 25, 26, 27, 28, 29, 30
December	2, 3, 4, 11, 12, 13, 14, 15, 16, 18, 19, 20, 21, 23, 24, 25

Travel

Setting out on a holiday or adventurous journey is exciting. Here are the most favourable times for doing this. Travel on the following dates is likely to give you a sense of fulfilment:

January	15
February	15, 16, 18, 19, 20, 21
March	16, 17, 18, 21, 22, 23
April	19, 24, 25, 26, 27
May	16, 17, 18, 21, 22
June	17, 18, 19, 20, 21, 24, 25
July	21, 22, 23, 24, 25
August	19
September	9, 21, 22
October	18, 19, 20, 21, 22
November	7, 16, 17, 18
December	6, 14, 16, 19, 20

Beauty and grooming

Believe it or not, cutting your hair or nails has a powerful effect on your body's electromagnetic energy. If you cut your hair or nails at the wrong time of the month, you can reduce your level of vitality significantly. Use these dates to ensure you optimise your energy levels by staying in tune with the stars.

Hair and nails

January	1, 2, 3, 4, 5, 6, 7, 8, 11, 12, 13, 14, 15, 18, 19, 20, 21, 22, 25, 26, 27
February	3, 4, 5, 7, 8, 15, 16, 17, 18, 19, 22, 23, 24, 25
March	2, 3, 4, 6, 7, 8, 14, 15, 21, 22
April	1, 2, 3, 4, 5, 10, 11, 12, 17, 18, 19, 20, 21, 22, 23, 28, 29, 30
May	1, 2, 3, 4, 5, 7, 8, 9, 10, 11, 12, 13, 15, 16, 17, 18, 25, 26 27, 28, 29, 30
June	4, 5, 11, 12, 14, 15, 16, 24, 25
July	1, 2, 3, 8, 9, 12, 13, 14, 21, 22, 28, 29, 30
August	1, 2, 5, 6, 17, 18, 19, 25, 26
September	1, 2, 6, 7, 14, 15, 21, 22, 23, 24, 28, 29, 30
October	3, 4, 11, 12, 18, 19, 20, 25, 26, 27, 28, 29, 30
November	7, 8, 9, 14, 15, 16, 22, 23, 24, 25, 26, 27
December	5, 6, 12, 13, 19, 20, 21, 22, 23, 24, 25

Therapies, massage and self-pampering

January	6, 7, 13, 14, 15, 18, 19, 20, 21
February	2, 3, 9, 11, 14
March	1, 9, 14, 16, 17, 20, 23, 29
April	4, 5, 6, 10, 11, 12, 13, 17, 25, 26
May	2, 3, 7, 8, 9, 10, 11, 14, 15, 16, 17, 22, 23, 24, 31
June	3, 5, 12, 18, 19, 26, 27
July	4, 7, 8, 9, 10, 16, 23, 28, 29, 30, 31
August	3, 4, 5, 6, 7, 13, 20, 21, 24, 25, 26, 27, 28, 31
September	2, 17, 21, 28, 29

October	13, 14, 15, 18, 19, 21, 25, 26, 27, 28
November	2, 3, 9, 11, 14, 15, 16, 17, 21, 24, 29
December	7, 12, 13, 14, 15, 18, 19, 20, 22, 26, 27, 28, 29

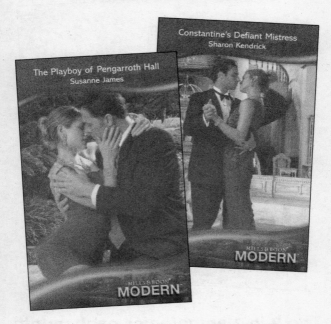

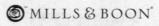

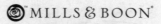

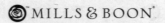